Elements and the Periodic Table

What Things Are Made Of

BY
THEODORE S. ABBGY

COPYRIGHT © 2001 Mark Twain Media, Inc.

ISBN 1-58037-166-3

Printing No. CD-1387

Mark Twain Media, Inc., Publishers
Distributed by Carson-Dellosa Publishing Company, Inc.

Table of Contents

The Teacher's Guide: *Introduction*

Most periodic tables available for middle-grade students contain complex information that is taught to high school students and even college students. This information is not necessary when middle-school students are being introduced to the periodic table. The periodic tables in this book are designed to introduce the periodic table to middle-school students. The tables contain information such as atomic number and symbol; however, they leave out more complex ideas, such as atomic mass and valences. These ideas can be taught later in a student's high school or college education.

It is the intent of this book to present an introductory unit on elements and the periodic table. This book is written in a sequential form and can be used as a unit itself, or individual pages can be used to supplement any element unit.

Most of the materials in this book have been used in heterogeneous, multicultural, urban, and suburban classrooms. These activities are designed to teach the students to understand the periodic table and to have fun learning. These materials rely on a whole host of teaching techniques to motivate most of the learners in the classroom.

This book contains activities, transparency masters, quizzes, tests, rubrics, and grading sheets designed to teach students how to use the periodic table and how elements affect their lives.

1. What Are Elements?

This chapter contains an easy-to-use periodic table, activities designed to familiarize the students with elements, a comparison of elements to other forms of matter, graphing activities, a brief history of elements and the periodic table, time line activities to go with the brief history, and a chapter quiz.

2. Uses of Elements

The activities in this chapter are centered around a rather lengthy and comprehensive list of the elements and their uses, in the form of a booklet. The *Uses of the Elements* booklet is accompanied by activities that include classroom construction of a wall-size periodic table, as well as activities designed to demonstrate to students how the elements affect their lives.

3. Element Symbols

Students are introduced to the rules for writing atomic symbols. In this chapter, activities are included to aid the students in the memorization of 25 of the elements and their symbols.

The Teacher's Guide: *Introduction*

4. The Organization of the Periodic Table

In this section, students are given a brochure that teaches all of the things that can be found on the periodic table shown on the first student page of this book. A study guide follows, which helps students to understand the brochure. Students may participate in a lab that will show how the salts of two of the element families react to ammonium compounds. There is also an activity that lets each cooperative group draw a poster of an assigned family.

At the end of the chapters, an element game is presented to help students review the information they have learned. A comprehensive test over the elements and the periodic table is provided as well.

The best way to utilize the materials in this book is as a self-contained unit; all or most of the pages may be used. However, teachers may choose to use selected pages to supplement textbook chapters or teacher-made units. Many of the activities can be used in cooperative groups. Some activities can be done as individual classroom assignments or as homework. Most of the activities in this book are flexible enough to be used in the method that best suits the composition of the class, as well as the personality of the teacher.

The Teacher's Guide: *Teaching the Periodic Table*

Cooperative Learning

Many of the activities in this book are designed to be done in cooperative groups. Some of the activities in this book can be done individually or in cooperative groups. It all depends on the makeup of the class and the teacher's comfort with cooperative learning.

The activities in this book work best with eight-, three- or four-person groups. It is recommended that the teacher select the members of the group. However, certain activities work well with student-made groups.

When creating cooperative groups, teachers should consider a number of factors, such as conduct, creativity, intelligence, attitude, leadership abilities, gender, and maturity levels of the students. Mixing students by the factors listed above can help groups function more effectively.

Conduct, creativity, gender, and leadership qualities should be given major consideration when teachers are assigning cooperative groups. Poorly-behaved students need to be evenly distributed among the cooperative groups in a class. There should be one creative student assigned to each group. There should be one student with good leadership qualities assigned to each group. Boys and girls should be evenly distributed among the groups.

Social Skills

When teaching middle-school students, it is to the teacher's advantage to have three to five social skills rules so the students can work together effectively as a cooperative group. The purpose of these social skills rules is to keep the students on task, to keep everybody participating at all times, to make sure the students can give their attention to the teacher when needed, to keep the students pacing themselves so the task can be completed in the allowed time, and to keep the classroom from getting too noisy. There are several social skills that can be taught to students to accomplish these purposes. Social skills assessments are available on pages 8 and 9 of this book. Some suggested social skills rules for the purpose of this book include:

1. Use library voices - This should help keep the noise level tolerable.
2. Stay on task - This will remind the students to keep working on the activity.
3. Everyone participates - This will remind groups to keep everybody involved in the activity.
4. Attend to the teacher - Students need to be reminded that when the teacher needs the attention of the entire class, they need to stop what they are doing and pay close attention.
5. Pace yourself - All too often students spend too much time on one part of the activity. The students need to be given clear directions as to when the activity needs to end, and it is necessary for them to meet that time line.

The Teacher's Guide: *Teaching the Periodic Table*

Cross-Curricular Learning

An effective middle-school team often engages in cross-curricular learning. Elements and the periodic table provide a vehicle for cross-curricular learning. Since the discovery of the elements is rooted in history, the science teacher and the history teacher can work together with the historical development of the periodic table. Elements have been discovered in many countries. The science teacher and the geography teacher may want to get together with this. The health teacher can get involved with the elements that are needed in the body and the foods we need to eat to get these elements. The science and math teachers on a team can get together and teach data collection and graphing.

This book is designed to make cross-curricular learning easy for the teachers and the students on a middle-school team.

Multiple Intelligences

We as science teachers are guilty of believing that all students are logical/mathematical thinkers. We need to be reminded from time to time that students come as seven types of thinkers, not just one. The seven intelligences include:

1. Verbal/Linguistic
2. Logical/Mathematical
3. Visual/Spatial
4. Body/Kinesthetic
5. Musical/Rhythmic
6. Interpersonal
7. Intrapersonal

Teachers may want to survey their classes to find out which intelligences are most prominent and which intelligences need to be stressed. Multiple intelligence surveys are available today. This book stresses the logical/mathematical intelligence; however, many of the activities can be adapted to other intelligences. Here are some suggestions of how to adapt some of the activities to the multiple intelligences.

Verbal/Linguistic

In many of the cooperative learning activities, verbal/linguistic learners will discuss what they have learned with other members of the group. In the Create a Phrase activity on page 70, verbal/linguistic learners may want to present their phrases to the class. In the Families of Elements Poster Activity on page 89, have the groups present and explain their posters. Verbal/linguistic learners will be happy to explain what the group has done. In the Element Game on page 100, verbal/linguistic learners will thrive on answering the questions on the question cards.

The Teacher's Guide: *Teaching the Periodic Table*

Logical/Mathematical

Most of the activities in this book stress logical/mathematical learning. Many of the graphing activities, time line activities, symbol activities, using data activities, and periodic table activities lend themselves to the logical/mathematical learner. Very few adaptations need to be made to teach the logical/mathematical learner.

Visual/Spatial

The periodic table itself is a visual. Time lines and graphs also help the visual/spatial learner become successful in class. The transparency master on page 17 can be adapted as a visual/spatial activity. Teachers could have students make visuals on common elements, compounds, and mixtures used in school, at home, at the mall, at restaurants, or at hospitals. An adaptation to the activity called Periodic Pictures Element Uses on page 43 can be made for visual/spatial learners. Here teachers can assign bonus points to students who can make more visuals to illustrate uses of elements. For the Create a Table Activity on page 45, have the visual/spatial learners do the cutting and pasting of the final periodic table.

Body/Kinesthetic

The Element, Compound, or Mixture Activity on page 18 can be adapted to the body/kinesthetic learner. Have these students do demonstrations to show the differences between elements, mixtures, and compounds. Body/kinesthetic learners should be given an opportunity to demonstrate uses of elements shown in the *Uses of the Elements* booklet. Here students could brush their teeth to show the use of fluorine, do jumping jacks to show the use of oxygen, show a baseball or golf swing to show a use of titanium, and many other physical activities to demonstrate the uses of elements.

Musical/Rhythmic

Students can make up songs, raps, or poems that tell what elements are, show the uses of elements, show the element symbols, and show how the periodic table is organized. Students will have fun recording their works on audio or video cassettes. Have the students who play brass instruments bring them to class and demonstrate how they work and explain why copper alloys are used to make these instruments. These students may want to play a tune on their instruments to demonstrate the sounds made.

Interpersonal

Interpersonal learners will benefit from cooperative learning. They will explain situations to the other members of the group. While checking activities in class, interpersonal learners will volunteer explanations of answers if given the opportunity.

The Teacher's Guide: *Teaching the Periodic Table*

Intrapersonal

One adaptation that can be made to this book for intrapersonal learners is keeping logs of elements that are used in everyday life. Students will be amazed at how many times they use elements. Have students write a story similar to Harlan's Day on page 60, but as applied to themselves. Here students will intrapersonalize elements in their lives. This same activity can be applied to mixtures, compounds, and element families. The time lines provide an excellent opportunity for students to intrapersonalize their educations. Have students make a time line of their lives. This intrapersonal time line can show accomplishments from their first words to graduation from elementary school. Have the students include photographs of themselves as babies, toddlers, preschoolers, and elementary students. The photographs can be placed on the appropriate places in the time line.

Assessment

Most of the activities in this book are assessment tools of one kind or another. Quizzes are provided on pages 27, 60, 72, 73, 74, and 97. Tests are provided on pages 75 and 115. Rubrics are provided on pages 24, 69, and 90. Grading sheets are provided on pages 19, 29, 117, and 118.

Portfolios can also be used as assessment tools. Students can make collective portfolios of all their work for the periodic table unit or for each chapter. Students can also make showcase portfolios of works selected by the teacher or the students. Several portfolio assessments and cooperative learning assessments have been provided on pages 8-11.

Using the Assessment Sheets

Page 8 - Social Skills Teacher Assessment. This assessment is designed for teacher use only. This sheet can be used with any group activity to assess how a group performs its social skills. Page 8 can be photocopied and cut in half. The teacher should write in the social skills that are being stressed during that particular group activity. The teacher should visit each group twice during that activity. Every time the teacher visits a group, he or she will assign that group 0-5 points for each social skill, based on how well the members of the group conform to the social skills rules for that activity. Use the following grading scale:

    5 = Excellent
    4 = Good
    3 = Needs Improvement
    2 = Poor
    1 = Social skill violated from time to time
    0 = Social skill violated most of the time

Teachers can assign the group a social skills grade or they can add the 50 possible points earned on the social skills to the grade of the activity itself.

The Teacher's Guide: *Teaching the Periodic Table*

Page 9 - Social Skills Student Evaluation. This assessment is designed for students to evaluate their own performance in groups. Teachers may want to give each student one of these sheets, have them fill out the social skills, and evaluate the group's performance on a particular activity. Teachers may also want to assign an evaluator for each cooperative group and only allow those students to complete the sheet. Either way, teachers will get an idea of how each group is doing as far as social skills are concerned.

Page 10 - Showcase Portfolio. This assessment applies to any unit. Have the students pick five activities completed during the unit that they think of as their best work. In the spaces provided on the cover sheet, students will write the names of the activities and the reasons why they chose those activities to be put in their showcase portfolios. Teachers should grade students' work based on the work and the reasons given. Here is a suggested grading scale:

    5 = Excellent
    4 = Good
    3 = Needs Improvement
    2 = Poor
    1 = Insufficient work or reasons given
    0 = Nonexistent

Page 11 - Collective Portfolio. This assessment applies to any unit. It is best to give this to the students on the day the unit starts; each activity can then be recorded as it is received. Space for 26 activities has been provided. Do not be concerned if all 26 spaces are not used up. At the end of the unit, the students should arrange their papers in the order they are listed on the table of contents, and staple their papers to the table of contents.

The Teacher's Guide: *Social Skills Teacher Assessment*

Group # _____ Period _____   Name _____

Activity _____   Name _____

Social Skills Teacher Assessment   Name _____

Social Skill	First Visit (5)	Second Visit (5)	Total (10)
_____	_____	_____	_____
_____	_____	_____	_____
_____	_____	_____	_____
_____	_____	_____	_____
_____	_____	_____	_____
_____	_____	_____	_____

Total (50) _____

Group # _____ Period _____   Name _____

Activity _____   Name _____

Social Skills Teacher Assessment   Name _____

Social Skill	First Visit (5)	Second Visit (5)	Total (10)
_____	_____	_____	_____
_____	_____	_____	_____
_____	_____	_____	_____
_____	_____	_____	_____
_____	_____	_____	_____
_____	_____	_____	_____

Total (50) _____

The Teacher's Guide: *Social Skills Student Evaluation*

Group # _____ **Period** _____   **Name** _____

Activity _____   **Name** _____

Social Skills Student Evaluation   **Name** _____

Directions: For this activity, write the five social skills stressed by your teacher in the space provided below. Circle the number that best relates to how your group performed on each social skill. Then total your score. Be honest so your teacher can help you to become a better group.

Points	Behaviors
5	Excellent! Your group mastered this skill.
4	Good job! Your group did a good job of following this skill.
3	Average! Your group may not have followed this skill all the time, but it tried.
2	Needs work! It was a rare occasion when this skill was followed.
1	Needs lots of work! Most of the time this skill was not followed.
0	A disaster! Students in your group never followed this skill.

1. _____   0 1 2 3 4 5

2. _____   0 1 2 3 4 5

3. _____   0 1 2 3 4 5

4. _____   0 1 2 3 4 5

5. _____   0 1 2 3 4 5

Total _____

Write any comments or concerns that your group has in the space below or on the back of this page. Include comments or concerns about the activity or the social skills. Word the comments in such a way that your teacher can help you overcome any difficulties.

_____

_____

The Teacher's Guide: *Showcase Portfolio*

Showcase Portfolio   Name _____

Unit _____   Date _____ Hour _____

Directions: Pick five completed unit activities that show your best work. Assemble them, using this page as a cover sheet. In the spaces provided below, write the name of the activity and give reasons why this is your best work.

<u>Teacher Use Only</u>

1. Name of Activity _____   0 1 2 3 4 5
    Reason you chose this activity

    _____

    _____

2. Name of Activity _____   0 1 2 3 4 5
    Reason you chose this activity

    _____

    _____

3. Name of Activity _____   0 1 2 3 4 5
    Reason you chose this activity

    _____

    _____

4. Name of Activity _____   0 1 2 3 4 5
    Reason you chose this activity

    _____

    _____

5. Name of Activity _____   0 1 2 3 4 5
    Reason you chose this activity

    _____

    _____

Total (25) _____

The Teacher's Guide: *Collective Portfolio*

Collective Portfolio

Unit _____

Name _____

Date _____ **Hour** _____

Directions: Gather all of your papers from this unit and assemble them in order by date. Complete this table of contents and staple it to your papers.

Table of Contents

Page #	Title	Date
____ 1.	_____	_____
____ 2.	_____	_____
____ 3.	_____	_____
____ 4.	_____	_____
____ 5.	_____	_____
____ 6.	_____	_____
____ 7.	_____	_____
____ 8.	_____	_____
____ 9.	_____	_____
____ 10.	_____	_____
____ 11.	_____	_____
____ 12.	_____	_____
____ 13.	_____	_____
____ 14.	_____	_____
____ 15.	_____	_____
____ 16.	_____	_____
____ 17.	_____	_____
____ 18.	_____	_____
____ 19.	_____	_____
____ 20.	_____	_____
____ 21.	_____	_____
____ 22.	_____	_____
____ 23.	_____	_____
____ 24.	_____	_____
____ 25.	_____	_____
____ 26.	_____	_____

Total _____

The Teacher's Guide: *The Supply List*

The following supply list will be needed for the activities in this book. The quantities are based on one class of 32 students. For group activities, the quantities are based on one class of 32 students divided into 8 groups of 4 students each. Since most middle-grade science teachers have more than one class, teachers may need more of some of the consumable supplies.

Page 16 - 32 periodic tables

Page 18 - 32 periodic tables

Page 19 - Colored pencils, highlighters, or markers; metric rulers

Page 22 - Colored pencils

Page 23 - Metric rulers; paper - 35 cm x 11 cm (half of a legal sheet cut long ways will do); colored pencils

Pages 27-29 - Metric rulers; periodic table; the History of the Elements sheet (pages 20 and 21); What Are Elements? transparency master (page 17); colored pencils, highlighters, or markers

Page 43 - The *Uses of the Elements* booklet (pages 32–42)

Page 44 - The *Uses of the Elements* booklet (pages 32–42)

Page 45 - Periodic cut-outs (pages 47–57); scissors; tape; colored pencils or markers; Elements Uses booklet (pages 32–42); periodic table; transparency master on page 46; poster board or bulletin board paper (at least 30″ x 40″)

Page 58 - The *Uses of the Elements* booklet (pages 32-42)

Pages 59-61 - The *Uses of the Elements* booklet (pages 32-42); rulers; colors

Page 64 - Periodic table

Pages 65-66 - Periodic table; colored pencils or highlighters

Page 67 - Elements and symbols cards (page 68), 25-3″ x 5″ index cards, scissors, tape, colored paper

Pages 70-76 - Periodic table

Pages 82-83 - Periodic table; *Organizing the Elements* brochure (pages 79-81)

Pages 84–86 - Safety goggles; aprons; 20mL of 0.5M solutions of ammonium carbonate, ammonium phosphate, barium chloride, calcium chloride, lithium chloride, potassium chloride, sodium chloride, and strontium chloride; six test tubes; test tube rack; eight Barnes bottles; distilled water; periodic table

Pages 87-88 - Periodic table; lab sheets (pages 85-86)

Page 89 - Markers; rulers; poster paper; periodic table; resource information (pages 92-96); other resources (optional); booklet (pages 32-42)

Page 100 - Copier with enlarger and reducer; laminating machine; scissors; straight edge/ ruler

Pages 115-118 - Rulers; colored pencils; resources (if teacher desires)

Chapter 1: What Are Elements?: *The Teacher's Guide*

Page 15 - The Periodic Table of the Elements

This periodic table can be reproduced so that each student has his or her own copy, or it can be reproduced in a classroom set so copies are available in the classroom. Other periodic tables can be used with the activities in this book; however, this periodic table is designed to correspond with the activities in this book. This periodic table contains the element names, symbols, atomic numbers, families, and states of matter.

Page 16 - Getting To Know You—The Periodic Table

This worksheet can be done in groups, individually, or even as homework. Students are required to list 15 elements they can find on the periodic table that are familiar to them and tell one use for each of the 15 elements they listed. It's interesting, when the activity is completed, to ask students to offer one element and use from their lists. As an extension of this activity, teachers may offer extra credit to students who list more than 15 elements and their uses or for students who list more than one use for the elements on their list of 15.

Page 17 - Transparency Master

This overhead is designed to show the differences between elements, compounds, and mixtures. It also defines the periodic table and gives definitions and examples of elements, compounds, and mixtures. Some teachers may make just an overhead of this, while others may make a classroom set, and still others may make a copy for each student.

Page 18 - Element, Compound, or Mixture

Students will use the transparency master on page 17 and a periodic table to complete the worksheet. This activity can be done individually or in groups.

Page 19 - Where Are the Elements?

On this page, students are given the opportunity to impress their teachers with their graphing skills. The students will produce a graph showing the elements found in the human body. A grading area has been provided for the student to see how the graph will be graded and to make it easy for the teacher to evaluate the graph. Stress to the students the importance of making neat, clear, colorful, and correct bar graphs. This page is designed to show the students the elements that make up the body. As an extension for gifted students in your class or for students who correctly complete the assignment early, teachers may assign these students to construct pie graphs of the elements in the body. This activity is best done individually.

Pages 20-21 - The History of Elements and the Periodic Table

These pages can be read by student volunteers, individually by each student quietly, or students can take turns reading in their cooperative groups. Copies of these sheets can be made in classroom sets or for each student. These pages are designed to give the students a brief background on the history of the elements and the periodic table and can be used as a reference for some of the pages to follow.

Chapter 1: What Are Elements?: *The Teacher's Guide (cont.)*

Pages 22-24 - Time Lines

Setting up time lines can be difficult for students. Page 22 can be used as a teacher-guided activity. On page 22 the time line has been set up where 1 cm = 20 years. Students need only write the elements and their discovery dates in the proper place on the time line. On page 23, students are required to set up the time line themselves. Here they must make a scale, a title, a legend, and properly place the data on the time line. For page 23, students will need a ruler and a strip of paper - 35 cm x 11 cm (a sheet of legal-size paper cut in half the long way will do). A grading rubric for page 23 is provided on page 24. If the teacher chooses to use the rubric, the students should be provided with a copy of the rubric before they begin drawing the time line. Encourage the students to use illustrations and color on their time lines. As an extension for this activity, teachers may want to have students construct a time line of the significant events that have happened in their lives. Other extensions for this activity may include redrawing the time line on page 23 on a larger piece of paper, adding-machine tape, continuous-feed computer paper, or poster board. In addition, teachers may want students to draw time lines of some of the events listed on the reference on pages 20-21. Time lines are best done individually.

Pages 25-26 - Naming the Elements

This matching activity is designed to give the students an idea of how the elements are named. Stress to the students that some letters are missing in the element column on page 25, so the two messages could be constructed on page 26. This worksheet is best done individually. This activity is easily graded, because if the students have the messages written correctly, they will have the matching correct. This activity can be easily graded in class by having the students trade papers and the teacher read the answers. An extension for this activity can include having the students make up their own messages about elements and the periodic table.

Pages 27-29 - Quiz

To do this quiz, teachers may choose to allow the students to use a periodic table, the transparency master on page 17, the history reference on pages 20-21, their textbooks, and any papers in their portfolios, journals, notebooks, or science logs. This quiz provides students with writing and matching exercises; they must make a time line of Marie Curie's life; and they must make a bar graph of the dissolved materials in seawater. Although the graphing section has a grading table, the other sections may be time-consuming and tedious to check. It is suggested that Parts II and III be checked in class by having students trade papers and the teacher reading the answers.

Chapter 1: What Are Elements?: *The Periodic Table of the Elements*

The Periodic Table of the Elements

Legend:
- 1 — Alkali Metals
- 2 — Alkaline Earth Metals
- 3–12 — Transition Metals
- 13–16 — BCNO Groups
- 17 — Halogens
- 18 — Noble Gases

Gas – H, He, N, O, F, Ne, Cl, Ar, Kr, Xe, Rn

Liquid – Br, Hg

Solid – All Others

Group																	
1	2	3	4	5	6	7	8	9	10	11	12	13	14	15	16	17	18

1 H Hydrogen																	2 He Helium
3 Li Lithium	4 Be Beryllium											5 B Boron	6 C Carbon	7 N Nitrogen	8 O Oxygen	9 F Fluorine	10 Ne Neon
11 Na Sodium	12 Mg Magnesium											13 Al Aluminum	14 Si Silicon	15 P Phosphorus	16 S Sulfur	17 Cl Chlorine	18 Ar Argon
19 K Potassium	20 Ca Calcium	21 Sc Scandium	22 Ti Titanium	23 V Vanadium	24 Cr Chromium	25 Mn Manganese	26 Fe Iron	27 Co Cobalt	28 Ni Nickel	29 Cu Copper	30 Zn Zinc	31 Ga Gallium	32 Ge Germanium	33 As Arsenic	34 Se Selenium	35 Br Bromine	36 Kr Krypton
37 Rb Rubidium	38 Sr Strontium	39 Y Yttrium	40 Zr Zirconium	41 Nb Niobium	42 Mo Molybdenum	43 Tc Technetium	44 Ru Ruthenium	45 Rh Rhodium	46 Pd Palladium	47 Ag Silver	48 Cd Cadmium	49 In Indium	50 Sn Tin	51 Sb Antimony	52 Te Tellurium	53 I Iodine	54 Xe Xenon
55 Cs Cesium	56 Ba Barium	57 La Lanthanum	72 Hf Hafnium	73 Ta Tantalum	74 W Tungsten	75 Re Rhenium	76 Os Osmium	77 Ir Iridium	78 Pt Platinum	79 Au Gold	80 Hg Mercury	81 Tl Thallium	82 Pb Lead	83 Bi Bismuth	84 Po Polonium	85 At Astatine	86 Rn Radon
87 Fr Francium	88 Ra Radium	89 Ac Actinium	104 Rf Rutherfordium	105 Db Dubnium	106 Sg Seaborgium	107 Bh Bohrium	108 Hs Hassium	109 Mt Meitnerium	110 Uun Unununilium	111 Uuu Unununium	112 Uub Ununbium						

Lanthanides:

58 Ce Cerium	59 Pr Praseodymium	60 Nd Neodymium	61 Pm Promethium	62 Sm Samarium	63 Eu Europium	64 Gd Gadolinium	65 Tb Terbium	66 Dy Dysprosium	67 Ho Holmium	68 Er Erbium	69 Tm Thulium	70 Yb Ytterbium	71 Lu Lutetium

Actinides:

90 Th Thorium	91 Pa Protactinium	92 U Uranium	93 Np Neptunium	94 Pu Plutonium	95 Am Americium	96 Cm Curium	97 Bk Berkelium	98 Cf Californium	99 Es Einsteinium	100 Fm Fermium	101 Md Mendelevium	102 No Nobelium	103 Lr Lawrencium

Name: _____ Date: _____

Chapter 1: What Are Elements?: *Getting to Know You—The Periodic Table*

Directions:
1. Study the periodic table.
2. Make a list of 15 elements that you recognize.
3. Write one use for each element that you list.

Example:

Aluminum - Used to make soda cans.

Your list:

1. _____

2. _____

3. _____

4. _____

5. _____

6. _____

7. _____

8. _____

9. _____

10. _____

11. _____

12. _____

13. _____

14. _____

15. _____

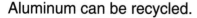

Aluminum can be recycled.   Aluminum is used for foil and cookware.

Chapter 1: What Are Elements?: *Transparency Master*

What Are Elements?

Elements are pure substances made of only one kind of atom.
Atoms are tiny structures found in all matter.
Most substances contain many different atoms.
Only the elements contain only one kind of atom.

ELEMENTS

1. One kind of atom
2. Pure
3. Separated in nuclear reactions

COMPOUNDS

1. Two or more kinds of atoms chemically bonded
2. Pure
3. Separated in chemical reactions

MIXTURES

1. Two or more elements or compounds physically together
2. Not pure
3. Separated in physical reactions

Aluminum
Soda Can

Gold
Jewelry

Water
Hydrogen and Oxygen

Salt
Sodium and Chlorine

Italian Dressing

The Periodic Table of the Elements

The periodic table was first constructed in 1869 to organize the elements by their properties. The periodic table in this book shows 112 elements. It organizes them by their families, atomic numbers, and many other properties.

Name: _____   Date: _____

Chapter 1: What Are Elements?: *Element, Compound, or Mixture*

Directions: Use the periodic table to identify the following substances as elements, compounds, or mixtures. Place the correct letter on the blank next to each substance.

E. Elements   **C. Compounds**   **M. Mixtures**

_____ 1. Gold   _____ 11. Paper

_____ 2. Salad Dressing   _____ 12. People

_____ 3. Aluminum Cans   _____ 13. Coins

_____ 4. Salt   _____ 14. Ammonia

_____ 5. Water   _____ 15. Air

_____ 6. Seawater   _____ 16. Soap

_____ 7. Vinegar   _____ 17. Soup

_____ 8. Wood   _____ 18. Silver

_____ 9. Rocks   _____ 19. Milk

_____ 10. Plastic   _____ 20. Copper

Directions: Make a list of five additional items that are familiar to you in each category of matter shown below.

Elements   **Compounds**   **Mixtures**

1. _____   1. _____   1. _____

2. _____   2. _____   2. _____

3. _____   3. _____   3. _____

4. _____   4. _____   4. _____

5. _____   5. _____   5. _____

Directions: Study the periodic table and make the following lists of elements.

Gases   **Transition Metals**   **Nonmetals**

1. _____   1. _____   1. _____

2. _____   2. _____   2. _____

3. _____   3. _____   3. _____

4. _____   4. _____   4. _____

5. _____   5. _____   5. _____

Name: _____ Date: _____

Chapter 1: What Are Elements?: *Where Are the Elements?— The Body*

Background: Where are the elements? Elements are found nearly everywhere: in the air, the oceans, the earth, and the body. The most common element in the air is nitrogen, in the earth is oxygen, and in the body is hydrogen.

Directions: Study the chart below titled **Elements of the Body**. Make a bar graph of the percentages of those elements in the space below or on your own paper. Do not write in the grading area. The teacher will use this area to grade your graph. When you make a graph, be sure to plan it out, make a title, scale and label the axes, keep it neat, and graph it correctly. You may use drawings and color to make your graph look more pleasing.

Elements of the Body

Element	Abundance
Hydrogen	63.0%
Oxygen	25.5%
Carbon	9.5%
Nitrogen	1.4%
Others	0.6%

Grading Area
(Two points for each area)

Title	_____
Neatness	_____
Scale	_____
Labels	_____
Completeness	_____
Plan	_____
Graphed Correctly	_____
Total (14)	_____
Percent (100)	_____
Grade	A B C D F

Chapter 1: What Are Elements?: *The History of Elements and the Periodic Table*

Ancient Times

Some elements were known and used by ancient civilizations. These elements were:

Carbon (pre-history)
Sulfur (pre-history)
Copper (~5000 BCE)
Silver (~3000 BCE)
Gold (~3000 BCE)

Iron (~2500 BCE)
Tin (~2100 BCE)
Antimony (~1600 BCE)
Lead (~1000 BCE)

Alchemy to the First Periodic Table (1000–1869)

During this time, 52 elements were discovered. Many of these elements were discovered by alchemists. Alchemists were people who tried to combine science and magic. They tried to change lead into gold. They discovered and used the scientific method. A few elements that were discovered during this period were:

Arsenic (~1250)
Zinc (~1500)
Phosphorus (1669)
Platinum (~1700)
Nickel (1751)

Nitrogen (1755)
Oxygen (1774)
Chlorine (1774)
Aluminum (1825)

Enter the Periodic Table

The first periodic table was drawn by a Russian scientist named Dimitry Mendeleyev in 1869. Mendeleyev put all 62 known elements on the first periodic table, and even allowed enough space for over 20 elements that had not yet been discovered. Mendeleyev's first periodic table closely resembles the table we use today. He also arranged the elements in the order of their atomic numbers, just as we do today.

Chapter 1: What Are Elements?: *The History of Elements and the Periodic Table (cont.)*

Rare and Radioactive Elements (1869–1899)

Many rare and radioactive elements were discovered during this modern period. Rare elements are elements that occur in very small amounts on earth. Radioactive elements are elements that give off small particles. A few elements discovered during this period include:

Fluorine (1886)   Neon (1898)
Argon (1894)   Polonium (1898)
Helium (1895)   Radium (1898)
Krypton (1898)   Actinium (1899)

Rare, Radioactive, and Synthetic Elements (1900–present)

During this modern period in chemistry, 30 elements have been created or discovered so far. These 20th-Century elements are very rare on earth. Some of them are very radioactive. Many of them are not found on earth at all, but were created in a laboratory. These are called synthetic elements. Some of these rare, radioactive, and synthetic elements include:

Radon (1900)   Americium (1944)
Francium (1939)   Dubnium (1970)
Plutonium (1940)   Ununbium (1996)

The Future

More new elements may be created in the future. Some periodic tables today provide space for elements up to #118. Many scientists are wondering why we should create new elements. Synthetic elements are very radioactive, they decay very quickly, and they cannot be studied or used. Other scientists are creating more elements because they believe that a stable, usable element may be discovered. Some scientists have even predicted that element #114 may be stable. Who knows? Perhaps this stable element will be discovered in your lifetime.

Name: _____ Date: _____

Chapter 1: What Are Elements?: *Element Time Line Practice*

A number of events have happened in history that have shaped today's periodic table. A large number of these events have occurred in the last 400 years, most of them in the twentieth century. The biggest events have been the discovery and synthesizing of many new elements.

Directions: Below is a list of a few elements and their discovery dates. Put the discovery dates and the elements in the proper place on the time line at the bottom of this page. You may want to make a drawing on your time line showing a use for each element. Phosphorus has already been done for you.

Elements (Discovery Date)

Phosphorus (1669)	Silicon (1824)	Hafnium (1923)	Dubnium (1970)
Hydrogen (1766)	Fluorine (1886)	Plutonium (1940)	Meitnerium (1982)
Uranium (1789)	Helium (1895)	Lawrencium (1961)	Ununbium (1996)
Sodium (1807)	Radon (1900)		

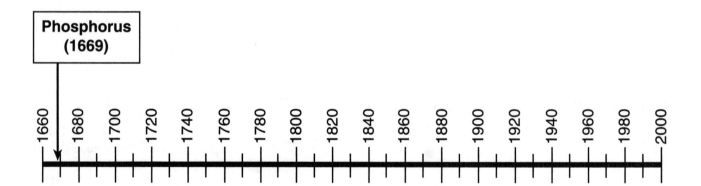

Scale: 1 cm = 20 years

Name: _____   Date: _____

Chapter 1: What Are Elements?: *Element Time Line Construction*

Purposes:
1. To construct a time line of the discovery of some elements.
2. To get a picture of how the periodic table was built over the last 350 years.

Materials:
   Metric Ruler, Paper ~35 cm x 11 cm, Colored Pencils

Procedures:
1. Plan out your time line. Remember, you have about 350 years to put on a piece of paper about 35cm long. Use your ruler.
2. Draw a line on your paper the length that you need. Use your ruler.
3. Make a scale. Draw small marks on your line showing the years. Use your ruler.
4. Label the marks. Write the years on the marks for the scale you have chosen.
5. Fill in the time line. Write each of the elements and their dates of discovery in the proper place on your time line.
6. Show a use. Draw a picture on the time line that shows a use for each element. Use your colored pencils.
7. Make an appropriate title for your time line and write it at the top.
8. Make an appropriate scale for your time line and write it at the bottom.

Data:

Element	Date of Discovery	Use
Phosphorus	1669	Makes some toys glow
Platinum	1700	Makes dental instruments
Nickel	1751	Makes up 25% of a five-cent piece
Oxygen	1774	Makes rocket fuel
Potassium	1807	Makes liquid soap
Iodine	1811	Used to develop photo film
Aluminum	1825	Makes aluminum foil
Indium	1863	Used in nuclear power plants
Argon	1894	Used in light bulbs
Protactinium	1917	Radioactive
Americium	1944	Used in smoke detectors
Ununnilium	1944	Radioactive

Chapter 1: What Are Elements?: *Rubric for Time Line*

Neatness (5 Points)

5   The time line looks excellent. It has a clear and accurate scale and title. Each entry is clearly and correctly marked. Writing and drawings are very neat and clear. A ruler was clearly used.

4   The time line looks good. It has a clear and accurate scale and title. Each entry is clearly and correctly marked. Writing and drawings are neat and clear. A ruler was used.

3   The time line looks average. Scale, title, or entries may be unclear or missing. Writing or drawings may not be neat or clear. A ruler may not have been used.

0-2 The time line looks poor. It appears to have been sloppily done in order to finish quickly. Scales, drawings, title, and entries may be missing, messy, or unclear. Writing is difficult or impossible to read. A ruler was not used.

Total Neatness Points (out of 5)   _____

Completeness (5 Points)

5   All components of the time line were completed in the given amount of time.

4   One of the components was incomplete or missing.

0-3 More than one of the components is incomplete or missing.

Total Completeness Points (out of 5)   _____

Accuracy (5 Points)

5   All measurements and scales were accurately measured with a ruler. All entries on the time line were as close to the discovery date as possible.

4   Measurements and scales were closely measured with a ruler. All entries were as close to the discovery date as possible.

3   Measurements and scales were measured with a ruler. One measurement, scale, or entry may have been slightly off.

2   Many measurements, scales, and entries were off. A ruler was used.

0-1 A ruler was not used. No measurements were made.

Total Accuracy Points (out of 5)   _____

Planning (5 Points)

5   An excellent plan was used to make the time line. The entire sheet of paper was used. The time line was made to fit the paper.

4   A good plan was used to make the time line. Most of the paper was used.

3   An average plan was used. Parts of the paper were unused. The events appear crowded together.

0-2 A plan was difficult to see or nonexistent.

Total Planning Points (out of 5)   _____

Total Points (out of 20)   _____

Percent (out of 100)   _____

Final Grade on Time Line   A B C D F

Name: _____ Date: _____

Chapter 1: What Are Elements?: *Naming the Elements*

Directions: Elements are named after people, places, and things. Below, match the element names to the people, places, or things. Use each element once, then write the letters in the messages on the next page to decode them. Some letters have not been used because they do not fit into the messages.

People, Places, or Things

_____ 1. Named for Dubna, a city in Russia where many new elements were created

_____ 2. Named for Berkeley, a city in California where many new elements were created

_____ 3. Named after the state of California.

_____ 4. Named for Marie Curie's home country of Poland

_____ 5. Named after the country of Germany

_____ 6. Named after Pierre Curie's home country of France

_____ 7. Named after the planet Uranus

_____ 8. Named after Neptune

_____ 9. Named after the planet Pluto

_____ 10. Named after the continent of Europe

_____ 11. Named after Ernest Rutherford, who discovered the nucleus

_____ 12. Named after Glen Seaborg, an American who created many new elements

_____ 13. Named after the Danish scientist Neils Bohr

_____ 14. Named after Lise Meitner, who discovered fission with her nephew, Otto Frisch

_____ 15. Named after Marie and Pierre Curie, who discovered radiation

_____ 16. Named after the physicist Albert Einstein

_____ 17. Named after Enrico Fermi, who created the first controlled nuclear reaction

_____ 18. Named after Alfred Nobel, who developed dynamite

_____ 19. Named after the inventor of the cyclotron, Ernest Lawrence

_____ 20. Named after America

_____ 21. Named after Dimitry Mendeleyev, who created the first periodic chart

Elements

A. Americium   B. Berkelium   C. Bohrium   D. Californium
E. Curium   F. Dubnium   G. Einsteinium   H. Europium
I. Fermium   L. Francium   M. Germanium   N. Lawrencium
O. Meitnerium   P. Mendelevium   R. Neptunium   S. Nobelium
T. Plutonium   U. Polonium   V. Rutherfordium   W. Seaborgium
Y. Uranium

Name: _____   Date: _____

Chapter 1: What Are Elements?: *Naming the Elements (cont.)*

Hidden Messages:

1. __ __ __ __   __ __ __ __ __ __ __ __   __ __ __
   5 20 19 7   15 6 15 5 15 19 9 18   20 8 15

   __ __ __ __ __   __ __ __ __ __   __ __ __ __
   16 17 11 15 19   19 20 5 15 18   1 8 14 5

   __ __ __ __ __   __ __ __ __ __ __ __ __ __ __.
   14 9 10 15 8   6 20 19 16 4 20 16 15 18

2. __ __ __ __   __ __ __ __ __ __ __ __   __ __ __ __
   18 14 5 15   15 6 15 5 15 19 9 18   12 15 8 15

   __ __ __ __ __   __ __   __ __ __
   19 20 5 15 3   2 7   9 10 15

   __ __ __ __ __ __ __   __ __ __ __ __ __   __ __ __
   20 19 13 17 15 19 9   21 15 14 21 6 15   12 10 14

   __ __ __ __   __ __ __ __.
   4 18 15 3   9 10 15 5

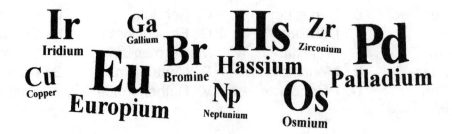

Name: _____ Date: _____

Chapter 1: What Are Elements?: *Quiz*

Part I. Using Words. Use the following words in one or two sentences to show that you under-stand their meanings.

1. Element, Periodic Table, Organized

    _____

    _____

    _____

    _____

2. Element, Compound, Mixture

    _____

    _____

    _____

    _____

Part II. Matching. Match the choices to the statements. Use each choice once.

_____ 3.	This element was known and used by ancient people.	A. Alchemists
_____ 4.	Two or more elements or compounds physically combined	B. Aluminum
_____ 5.	A substance that contains only one kind of atom	C. Argon
_____ 6.	An element that is used to make foil, cans, and cookware	D. Atom
_____ 7.	A substance with two or more different atoms chemically bonded together	E. Carbon
		F. Compound
_____ 8.	Elements that are made in a laboratory	G. Element
_____ 9.	These people tried to make lead into gold.	H. Mendeleyev
_____ 10.	A way of organizing elements by their physical properties	I. Mixture
_____ 11.	Tiny structures found in all matter	J. Periodic Table
_____ 12.	He drew the first periodic table of elements.	K. Radioactive Elements
_____ 13.	These elements give off small particles.	
_____ 14.	An element that is the gas in light bulbs	L. Synthetic Elements

Name: _____   Date: _____

Chapter 1: What Are Elements?: *Quiz (cont.)*

Part III. Element or Non-element. If it is an element, it is found on the periodic table. If it is not an element, you won't find it on the periodic table. Study the periodic table and identify each substance as:

E. Element   **N. Not an element**

Use the letter only and use the choices more than once.

_____ 15. Water   _____ 20. Gasoline

_____ 16. Tungsten   _____ 21. Salt

_____ 17. Gold   _____ 22. Tin

_____ 18. Pepper   _____ 23. Sugar

_____ 19. Iron   _____ 24. Chlorine

Part IV. Time Line. Marie Curie was a famous scientist. She discovered radioactivity, radium, and polonium. Below are some dates in her life. In the space provided below, draw a time line of her life.

1867 - Marie is born in Warsaw, Poland   1903 - Marie and Pierre win the Nobel Prize
1883 - Marie graduates from high school   1904 - Marie's daughter Eve is born
1893 - Marie earns a college degree in physics 1906 - Pierre is killed in an accident
1895 - Marie marries Pierre Curie   1911 - Marie wins her second Nobel Prize
1897 - Marie's daughter Irene is born   1934 - Marie dies of leukemia
1898 - Marie and Pierre discover two elements 1944 - Scientists create element 96 and
                                                     name curium after the Curies

Draw your time line in the space below.

Name: _____ Date: _____

Chapter 1: What Are Elements?: *Quiz (cont.)*

Part V. Graphing:

Background: Where are the elements? Elements are found nearly everywhere: in the air, the oceans, the earth, and the body. The most common element in the air is nitrogen, in the earth is oxygen, and in the body is hydrogen. The dissolved materials in ocean water also contain most elements. The most common element in these dissolved materials is chlorine.

Directions: Study the chart below titled **Dissolved Materials in Seawater**. Then make a bar graph of the percentage of those elements in the space below. Do not write in the grading area. The teacher will use that area to grade your graph. When you make your graph, be sure to plan it out, make a title, scale, and label the axes. Keep it neat and graph it correctly. You may use color and pictures on your graph to make it look more pleasing.

Dissolved Materials in Seawater

Element	Abundance
Chlorine	55.04%
Sodium	30.62%
Sulfur	7.68%
Magnesium	3.69%
Calcium	1.16%
Potassium	1.10%
Others	0.72%

Grading Area

(Two points for each area)

Title	_____
Neatness	_____
Scale	_____
Labels	_____
Completeness	_____
Plan	_____
Graphed Correctly	_____
Total (14)	_____
Percent (100)	_____
Grade	A B C D F

Chapter 2: Uses of Elements: *The Teacher's Guide*

Pages 32-42 - Uses of the Elements Booklet

Due to the length of this booklet, it is suggested that only classroom sets be used and teachers refrain from making copies for individual students. This booklet is designed as a classroom reference to be used with Chapter 3 and not to be read in its entirety.

Page 43 - Periodic Pictures

It is suggested that students be allowed to use the booklet on pages 32-42 as a reference to name one element used in each of the pictures on page 43. This activity can be done as a class activity or group activity, but should not be done as a homework assignment because of the availability of the booklet. It's fun when the activity is finished to call on students to offer their answers and see how many elements are used for each object in the activity. Grading this activity may be difficult because of the large number of elements that are used in each item. This is one activity that teachers may want to grade with an effort grade.

Page 44 - Places and Things

This activity can be done in class individually or in cooperative groups, but not as homework because of the availability of the reference booklet on pages 32-42. This activity requires students to list five elements that are used in each item on the activity sheet. This activity is difficult to grade because of the large number of elements used in each item. It is suggested that teachers call on students to offer answers they have written and an effort grade be given. It's fun to see how many elements are used for each item on the activity sheet. An extension of this activity can include having students who finish the assignment early to offer more items and list more elements for each item. Students can also be asked to list more elements used for the items present on the activity sheet.

Pages 45-57 - Create a Table—Group Work

The product of this group activity will be a huge, wall-size periodic table that graphically illustrates at least one use of each element. Page 45 contains the directions for the activity. A copy of this should be made for each group. Page 46 is a transparency master to be used by the teacher as an example of what each section will look like when going over the directions. All of the elements that have no uses are radioactive, and the radiation symbol may be drawn in the section for these elements. Pages 47-57 are the sections of the periodic table for each element. The sections are loosely placed in order by family. It is best to evenly distribute these pages to the groups so each group has roughly the same number of sections to design. Make a copy of each of these pages for each class that does this activity. The students should draw at least one use in each section for each element. When the students finish the elements they were assigned, they should tape them

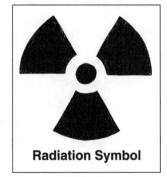

Radiation Symbol

Chapter 2: Uses of Elements: *The Teacher's Guide (cont.)*

in the proper place on a piece of poster board or bulletin-board paper. The poster board or bulletin-board paper should be at least 30" x 40". It can be slightly larger. The *Uses of the Elements* booklet on pages 32-42 should be made available for each group. Stress to the students the importance of neatness, clarity, and color when they are ready to do their drawings.

Page 58 - Crossword Puzzle

This page is designed as an enrichment page for the students in the groups that finish early. This can also be used as a review of the *Uses of Elements* booklet on pages 32-42. It may be easily checked with the students trading papers, and the teacher reading the answers.

Page 59 - Review

This activity will help students review some of the uses of the elements and help them to review by making use of the *Uses of the Elements* booklet on pages 32-42. The students should be allowed to use the booklet on the review.

Pages 60-61 - Quiz

For this quiz, the students should read a story called *Harlan's Day* and list ten elements that were used in the story. Allow the students to make use of the *Uses of the Elements* booklet on pages 32-42. The students will also need to make a comic strip on how one or more elements are used. Colored pencils may be used for this quiz, but are not necessary.

Chapter 2: Uses of Elements: *The Uses of the Elements Booklet*

Hydrogen
- Hydrogen was used to keep blimps and manned balloons aloft.
- Hydrogen combines with oxygen to form water.
- Hydrogen is used to make ammonia, fertilizer, margarine, and rocket fuel.
- Isotopes are used in nuclear reactions and hydrogen bombs.

Helium
- Helium is used today to fill blimps, manned balloons, toy balloons, and weather balloons.
- Scuba divers use a mixture of oxygen and helium to breathe.
- Helium was used to make the first gas lasers. Today gas lasers are used in bar code scanners.
- Helium is used as a liquid to cool particle accelerators.
- Helium is used by astronomers to eliminate space noise on their detectors.

Lithium
- Lithium combines with aluminum to make a light metal used in aircraft and spaceships.
- Lithium is used to make small batteries for cameras, calculators, and pacemakers.
- Lithium is used to purify air in spacecraft and submarines.
- Lithium is used in some soaps.
- Lithium is used to manufacture lubrication grease.
- Lithium is used as medication for bipolar disease.
- Isotopes are used to make hydrogen bombs.

Beryllium
- Beryllium is found naturally in gems. It gives emeralds and aquamarines their color.
- Beryllium is used to make X-ray tubes.
- Beryllium is used in rocket fuel and explosives.
- Isotopes are used for neutron sources in nuclear laboratories.

Boron
- Boron is used in water softeners.
- Boron is used as an eyewash.
- Boron is used to make heat-resistant glass, such

Boron (continued)
as Pyrex™, for baking dishes and measuring cups.
- Boron is used to make control rods in nuclear reactors.
- Boron is used for transistors in VCRs, computers, and calculators.

Carbon
- Many organic compounds are made from carbon.
- Many products such as petroleum and perfume are made from carbon.
- Natural diamonds are made of carbon.
- Graphite is made of carbon. Graphite is used in many products, such as pencils and synthetic diamonds.
- Carbon makes coal, which is used to make heat and electricity in some areas.
- Carbon is combined with oxygen to form carbon dioxide. Carbon dioxide is exhaled when we breathe, used in photosynthesis, used for carbonation in soft drinks, and used to make decaffeinated coffee.
- Dry ice is frozen carbon dioxide. It is used to freeze many things, such as ice cream.
- Carbon is used to remove pollutants from the air.
- Carbon is used in some inks, tires, and dry cells.
- Carbon combines with nitrogen to make cyanide, which is a very toxic poison.
- Isotopes are used to date rocks and fossils.

Nitrogen
- Nitrogen makes up 78% of air.
- Liquid nitrogen is used to freeze foods and biological specimens.
- Gaseous nitrogen is used to protect electronic materials.
- Nitrogen is used to store fruit for long periods of time. Apples stored in nitrogen gas can last 30 months without rotting.
- Nitrogen is used to pump oil from the ground.
- Nitrogen combines with carbon, hydrogen, and other elements to make protein.
- Nitrogen is used in the production of ammonia and fertilizer.

Chapter 2: Uses of Elements: *The Uses of the Elements Booklet*

Nitrogen (continued)
- Nitrogen combines with oxygen to form dangerous pollutants.
- Nitrogen is used to make nitrous oxide, a medicine that serves as a mild anesthetic.
- Nitrogen is used in whipped cream dispensers.
- Nitrogen is used to make dynamite and other explosives.
- Nitrogen is used to preserve canned food.
- Nitrogen is used in air bags in cars.
- Nitrogen is used in the PET scan, which is used in hospitals to detect brain dysfunction, schizophrenia, and Alzheimer's disease.

Oxygen
- We use oxygen to breathe.
- Every cell in the body needs oxygen.
- Oxygen makes ozone, which protects us from the harmful rays of the sun.
- Oxygen combines with hydrogen to make water.
- Oxygen combines with just about every element to make a family of compounds called oxides.
- Oxygen makes hydrogen peroxide, which is used as an industrial and cosmetic bleach and disinfectant.
- Oxygen is used as a liquid rocket fuel.

Fluorine
- Fluorine is added to many materials to lower the melting point.
- Fluorine is used to enrich uranium for use in nuclear power plants.
- Fluorine is added to water supplies and toothpaste to prevent cavities in teeth.
- Fluorine is used to make non-stick coating for pots and pans.
- Fluorine is used in spray cans.
- Fluorine, in the form of freon, is used in refrigerators and air conditioners.
- Fluorine is used in glass etchings.
- Isotopes are used in PET scans to produce cross-sectional pictures of portions of the body.

Neon
- Neon is used in lights because it glows in an orange or red color.
- Neon is used to liquefy air because of its low boiling point.

Sodium
- Sodium is used to transfer heat out of nuclear reactors.
- Sodium combines with chlorine to make table salt.
- Sodium is used in drain cleaner and oven cleaner.
- Sodium is used in several soaps because of its ability to dissolve grease.
- Sodium is used in baking soda.
- Sodium is used in medicine to provide relief for heartburn.
- Sodium is used in highway lights and fog lights because it glows yellow.
- Isotopes are used in medicine to trace movement in the body.

Magnesium
- When combined with aluminum, magnesium makes an alloy that is used in automobile parts, aircraft parts, power tools, lawnmower housings, and racing bikes.
- Magnesium is used in fireworks and flares because it gives off a bright white light when it burns.
- Magnesium is a valuable mineral for the proper nutrition of the human body.
- Magnesium is used in medicine to treat heartburn and skin rashes.
- Magnesium is used to treat leather and other fabrics to accept dye.

Aluminum
- Aluminum is used for aluminum foil.
- Aluminum is used in airplane wings.
- Aluminum is used in sandpaper and grinding tools.
- Aluminum is used to make fire bricks for ovens and furnaces.
- Aluminum is used to protect spark plugs and transistors.
- Aluminum is used in cosmetics for creams and lotions.

Chapter 2: Uses of Elements: *The Uses of the Elements Booklet*

Aluminum (continued)
- Aluminum makes several jewelry items such as rubies and sapphires.
- Aluminum can conduct electricity. It is used in wires, reflectors, resistors, antennas, and solar mirrors.
- When combined with copper, it is used in construction material.
- Aluminum is used to make drink cans, pots, and pans.
- Aluminum can be recycled.
- Aluminum is used in some doors, screens, and window frames.

Silicon
- Makes up gemstones such as opal, amethyst, agate, and jasper.
- Silicon makes up flint, which ancients used for tools and weapons.
- Ancients also used flint to start their fires.
- Silicon makes up quartz, which is used in clocks and watches.
- Quartz crystals are used for control devices for television and radio transmitters.
- Silicon is used in the production of glass, eyeglass lenses, and lenses for telescopes and microscopes.
- Pyrex™ is made from a combination of silicon and boron. Pyrex™ is used in baking dishes, measuring cups, beakers, and test tubes.
- Silicon is used to make ceramics, pottery, and china.
- Silicon is used in transistors and solar cells.
- Silicon is used in cosmetic surgery.
- Silicon chips are used in computers to store information.

Phosphorus
- Phosphorus is used to make materials glow, such as lights, glow-in-the-dark clocks, watches, and toys.
- Phosphorus is used in televisions to make the image.
- Phosphorus is an important nutrient in the body. It produces strong teeth and bones.

Phosphorus (continued)
- Phosphorus is used in laundry soaps and other detergents.

Sulfur
- Sulfur is used as a food preservative.
- Sulfur dioxide is used as an additive to wine and fruit.
- Sulfur dioxide is used to make paper.
- Sulfuric acid is a compound of sulfur that is used in fertilizers.
- Sulfuric acid is also used in car batteries and to remove rust from metals.
- Many sulfur products are used in making rubber, detergents, and paints.
- Sulfur is used in gunpowder.

Chlorine
- Chlorine was used in World War I as a poison gas.
- Chlorine is used as a germ killer in swimming pools and water supplies.
- Chlorine is used in bleach.
- Chlorine is used to make plastic pipes.
- Hydrochloric acid is a chlorine compound used for cleaning the rust off metal and is used in the stomach for digesting food.
- Chlorine is used in insecticides.
- Chlorine was used in air conditioners and refrigerators until recently when it was discovered that chlorine is a pollutant.

Argon
- Argon is the gas used to fill light bulbs and fluorescent bulbs.
- Argon is used as a gas in welding.
- Argon is used in Geiger counters, devices that sense radiation.
- Isotopes are used in dating rocks and fossils.

Potassium
- Potassium is a nutrient in plants. It is essential for plant growth. It is used in plant fertilizers.
- Potassium is used in scuba tanks to produce oxygen.

Chapter 2: Uses of Elements: *The Uses of the Elements Booklet*

Potassium (continued)
- Potassium is used to make batteries and liquid soap.
- Potassium is used in explosives and gunpowder.
- Potassium is used by humans as a valuable mineral needed by the body.
- Isotopes of potassium are used in dating rocks and fossils.

Calcium
- Calcium is a mineral needed in the human body for strong teeth and bones.
- Calcium is used as a medicine for heartburn.
- Calcium is used in building materials such as plaster and cement.
- Calcium was used in lighting stages for plays and concerts.
- Calcium is used in the production of iron.
- Calcium is a major component of marble, which is used for buildings and statues.

Scandium
- Scandium is used in aircraft construction
- Scandium is used in lights in football and baseball stadiums.
- Isotopes are used to refine petroleum products.

Titanium
- Titanium is used to house rockets and jet engines.
- Titanium is used to make bicycle frames.
- Titanium is used to make pins for bone surgery because it will not react with tissue.
- Titanium is used as a sunscreen.
- Titanium is used to give color to paint, paper, and plastics.
- Titanium was used by the navy in World War II as a smoke screen to hide from the enemy.

Vanadium
- Vanadium is used to make a hard steel used in engine parts and cutting tools.
- Oxides of vanadium are used as an oxygen source in making sulfuric acid.
- Vanadium steel is used in the structural parts of nuclear reactors.

Chromium
- Chromium is used as a protective and decorative coating for other metals. Its most common use for this purpose is for car bumpers.
- Chromium is used in the production of stainless steel.
- Chromium is used for coloring paints, cements, and plaster.
- Chromium gives rubies their red color. Rubies are used in jewelry and lasers.
- Chromium compounds are used for tanning leather and making high-quality recording tapes.

Manganese
- Manganese is used in hard steel for rifle barrels, bank vaults, railroad tracks, and bulldozers.
- Manganese is used to purify public water supplies.
- Manganese is used to brighten pottery and ceramics.
- Manganese compounds are used for batteries and flashlights.

Iron
- Iron is used in many products containing steel. Such uses include cars, tools, appliances, chains, and cooking utensils.
- Iron is used in buildings, bridges, and towers.
- Iron is used in magnets.

Cobalt
- Cobalt is used to make blue glass.
- Cobalt is used for high-speed drills and other cutting tools.
- Cobalt is used in some magnets.
- Cobalt is an essential nutrient in the body for healthy blood.
- Isotopes of cobalt are used in X-ray machines, for cancer treatment, and for sterilizing food.

Nickel
- Nickel makes up about 25% of the five-cent U.S. coin, the nickel.
- Nickel is used to coat other metals. For example, nickel is used to coat the propeller shafts of boats.

Chapter 2: Uses of Elements: *The Uses of the Elements Booklet*

Nickel (continued)
- Nickel is used in the heating elements in toasters and electric ovens.
- Nickel is used in magnets.
- Nickel is used in rechargeable batteries for calculators, computers, and electric shavers.

Copper
- Copper makes excellent water pipes and electrical wires.
- Copper is used in many of the U.S. coins, including coating the penny.
- Copper is used in buttons on police uniforms (that's where the term for police, *copper,* or *cop,* came from).
- The Statue of Liberty is made in part of copper.
- Copper is used in jewelry.
- Copper is combined with other metals to make alloys, such as brass and bronze.These alloys are used to make a variety of products including weapons, art pieces, and musical instruments, such as trumpets and trombones.
- Copper is used in paint for ships.

Zinc
- Zinc is used to coat and protect steel in items like garbage cans and fences.
- Zinc is used in batteries for flashlights, portable radios, and radio-controlled toys.
- Zinc is the chief metal in the penny, although it is coated with copper.
- Zinc is combined with copper to form the alloy called brass, which has many uses.
- Zinc compounds are used for many products, such as paint, sunscreen, photocopiers, television screens, and computer monitors.

Gallium
- Gallium is used as a metal in thermometers.
- Gallium is used in lasers.
- Gallium is used in the displays on watches and audio disc players.
- Gallium is being used to replace the silicon chips in high-power computers.
- Isotopes are used in cancer treatment.

Germanium
- Germanium chips are used in transistors and computers.

Arsenic
- Arsenic is used as a rat poison.
- Arsenic is used as a weed killer and insecticide.
- Arsenic was used by ancients as a yellow pigment. Its color is similar to that of gold.
- Arsenic is useful as a medicine for many diseases including skin diseases.
- Arsenic is used in computers and light-emitting diodes (LEDs). LEDs are used in watches and the displays on many electronic devices such as VCRs.

Selenium
- Selenium is used in robotics.
- Selenium is used as a light detector in cameras and light meters.
- Selenium is used in photocopiers.
- Studies have shown that small amounts of selenium in the diet can prevent cancer and heart disease.
- Selenium compounds are used in shampoos to prevent dandruff.

Bromine
- Bromine compounds are used to remove lead additives from gasoline.
- Bromine is used as a worm pesticide.
- Bromine is used in the production of photographic film.
- Bromine was used in the past as a sedative.

Krypton
- Krypton is a gas used in lights on signs and airport runway lights.
- Krypton is used in camera flashes and strobe lights.

Rubidium
- Rubidium is used in the manufacture of television picture tubes.
- Rubidium has other lab and technical uses.

Chapter 2: Uses of Elements: *The Uses of the Elements Booklet*

Strontium
- Strontium is used in fireworks and highway warning flares.
- Isotopes of strontium are used in detecting bone disease in the body. Some isotopes are also very dangerous and can cause bone disease.

Yttrium
- Moon rocks are high in yttrium.
- Compounds of yttrium are used in television picture tubes.
- Yttrium compounds are also used in laser cutting tools.
- Yttrium is used in superconductors that can elevate other metals at cold temperatures.
- Yttrium is used as a superconductor in trains. Yttrium will be used for this purpose in the future.

Zirconium
- Zirconium is used in space-vehicle parts.
- Zirconium is used in jewelry as a diamond substitute.
- Zirconium is used in control rods in nuclear reactors.

Niobium
- Niobium is used in the construction of nuclear reactors.
- Niobium is used as a superconductor in trains.
- Niobium is used in scanners in hospitals for detecting disease.
- Niobium is put into stainless steel used for aircraft, cutting tools, and spacecraft.

Molybdenum
- Molybdenum is used in steel to make car and plane engine parts, guns, and cannons.
- Isotopes of molybdenum are used to make technetium and used in hospitals for detecting disease.

Technetium
- Technetium is used to detect the damage to the heart during a heart attack.

Ruthenium
- Ruthenium is used to obtain hydrogen gas.
- Ruthenium is used in jewelry.
- Alloys of ruthenium are used for fountain pen points and electrical contacts.

Rhodium
- Rhodium is used in catalytic converters in cars to prevent pollution.
- Rhodium is used in car headlight reflectors.

Palladium
- Palladium is used in catalytic converters in cars to prevent pollution.
- Dentists use palladium for crowns on teeth.
- Palladium is used in jewelry.
- Palladium is used to purify hydrogen gas.
- Palladium is used to treat cancer tumors.

Silver
- Silver is used to make jewelry.
- Silver is used to coat mirrors.
- Silver is used to make utensils, such as forks and spoons.
- Silver makes photographic film and paper.
- Dentists use silver in tooth fillings.
- Silver is used to make coins.
- Silver is used to make wires.
- Silver compounds are used to develop photographs and in photochromic sunglasses.
- Compounds of silver are also used to seed clouds and make rain.

Cadmium
- Cadmium is used to coat and protect steel.
- Cadmium is poisonous to the human body. It can cause kidney failure and high blood pressure. It is found in tobacco leaves, so cigarettes and secondhand smoke have trace amounts of cadmium.
- Cadmium is used in batteries.
- Cadmium is used in control rods in nuclear power plants.
- Cadmium is used in overhead sprinkler systems in many factories, businesses, and homes.

Chapter 2: Uses of Elements: *The Uses of the Elements Booklet*

Indium
- Indium is used in transistors and photo cells.
- Indium foils are used to control nuclear reactions in nuclear reactors.

Tin
- Tin is used in foils and cans.
- Tin is used to make solder, which is used to join or patch metal.
- Tin is used to make electrical connections.
- Pewter is an alloy of tin that is used in utensils, art pieces, bowls, and plates.
- Other alloys of tin are used in printing and ceramics.

Antimony
- Antimony is used in matches.
- Antimony is used to make wastewater pipes.
- Antimony is added to the plastic that makes credit cards.
- Compounds of antimony are used in electrical insulation.

Tellurium
- Tellurium is added to other metals, such as copper or stainless steel, to make them easier to work with.

Iodine
- Iodine is used to kill germs in small cuts.
- Iodine tablets are used to purify water.
- Iodine is an important nutrient in the diet. The thyroid gland in the throat uses iodine. Iodine is often added to salt and animal feed for this purpose.
- When combined with silver, iodine is used in developing photographic film and cloud seeding.
- An isotope of iodine is used for testing the thyroid gland for disease.

Xenon
- Xenon is a gas used in lights and camera flashes.

Cesium
- Cesium is used by firefighters in areas where toxic fumes are released. Cesium reacts with water to produce the oxygen needed to breathe.
- Cesium is used in television picture tubes.
- Isotopes of cesium are used in atomic clocks.

Barium
- Compounds of barium are used to find diseases in the intestine.
- Barium metal is used to make spark plugs.
- Other compounds of barium are used in photographic paper, writing paper, and plastic.

Lanthanum
- Lanthanum is used in search lights, movie projectors, and studio lighting.
- Lanthanum isotopes are used in nuclear reactions.

Cerium
- Cerium compounds are used to line self-cleaning ovens and to polish lenses for cameras and telescopes.
- Cerium is used in searchlights and movie projectors.

Praseodymium
- Praseodymium is used in search lights and movie projectors.
- Compounds of praseodymium are used in car parts, jet parts, and paints as a yellow coloring.

Neodymium
- Neodymium is used to make colored glass used in welders' goggles and certain lasers.
- Neodymium is used to make some of the world's most powerful magnets. These magnets are used to tell if paper money is counterfeit.

Promethium
- Isotopes of promethium are used to produce heat in nuclear-powered batteries.
- Promethium isotopes are used to produce X-rays in portable X-ray machines.

Chapter 2: Uses of Elements: *The Uses of the Elements Booklet*

Samarium
- Samarium is used to make permeate magnets.
- Compounds of samarium are used in glass.

Europium
- Europium is used in color televisions and color computer monitors.
- Europium is used in fluorescent lamps.

Gadolinium
- Gadolinium is used to make steel.
- Gadolinium is used in color televisions and computer monitors.
- Gadolinium is used by airline inspectors to detect flaws in the aircraft.
- Gadolinium is used in X-ray screens.
- Isotopes of gadolinium are used in nuclear power plants for control rods as neutron absorbers.

Terbium
- Compounds of terbium are used in lasers.
- Terbium compounds are used to produce the green color in televisions and computer monitors.
- Alloys of terbium are used in compact discs and X-ray screens.

Dysprosium
- Dysprosium is used in color televisions and mercury lamps.
- Dysprosium is used to alloy compact discs to function more effectively.
- Isotopes of dysprosium are being considered for use in control rods in nuclear power plants as neutron absorbers.

Holmium
- Holmium is used as a yellow color in glass.

Erbium
- Erbium is used to color glass and enamel glass pink.
- Erbium is used in sunglasses and inexpensive jewelry.
- Erbium is used in telephone networks.
- Erbium is often added to metals to make them easier to work with.

Thulium
- Thulium is used in lasers.
- Thulium is used in portable X-rays for medical examinations and for detecting stress in metal machinery.

Ytterbium
- Ytterbium alloys are used to make stainless steel stronger for use in dental instruments.
- Ytterbium is used in synthetic jewelry.

Lutetium
- Isotopes of lutetium are used for determining the age of meteors and refining petroleum.

Hafnium
- Hafnium is used in control rods to control nuclear reactions in nuclear-powered submarines.

Tantalum
- Tantalum is used in medical surgery for hip joint replacement, plates for replacing parts of the skull, and screws and staples for holding together broken fragments of bones.
- Alloys of tantalum are used for aircraft parts, nuclear reactors, missiles, and medical and dental instruments.
- Tantalum is used in camera lenses.
- It is used in the circuits of cellular phones and small computers.

Tungsten
- Tungsten is used in light bulbs.
- Tungsten is used in television tubes and computer monitors.
- Compounds of tungsten are used on the blades of high-speed cutting tools.

Rhenium
- Rhenium is used in electrical switches
- Rhenium is used in instruments that measure very high temperatures.
- Rhenium is used in welding rods.
- Isotopes of rhenium are used to estimate the age of the universe.

Chapter 2: Uses of Elements: *The Uses of the Elements Booklet*

Osmium
- Alloys of osmium are used in fountain pen tips.
- Osmium is used in phonograph needles and electrical switches.

Iridium
- Iridium is used in hypodermic needles.
- Iridium is used in rocket engines.

Platinum
- Platinum is used to make jewelry.
- Pure platinum is used in refining oil, dental instruments, ceramics, and the electrical and electronics industries.
- Platinum metal is used in glass tubes and bulbs.
- Platinum is used in pacemakers for the human heart.
- Platinum is used in thin sheets to make missiles, jet engines, and razor blades.
- Platinum is used in car parts.
- Platinum compounds are used to treat cancer.

Gold
- Gold is used for money in the form of coins and bars.
- Gold is used by dentists to fill teeth.
- Gold is used to coat large glass plates and spacecraft.
- Gold is used to make jewelry, such as rings and necklaces.
- Isotopes of gold are used to treat certain types of cancer.

Mercury
- Mercury is used in the home for thermometers, barometers, thermostats, silent switches, and fluorescent bulbs.
- Mercury vapor is used in street lights and security lights.
- Mercury is used to refine ores containing gold.
- Mercury compounds are used as pesticides because they kill fungus and insects.
- Mercury is used for making blasting caps.
- Mercury is used in batteries.

Thallium
- Thallium was used to treat skin conditions.
- Thallium was used in rat poison and as an insecticide, but because it is so toxic, it has been banned from use in the United States.
- Thallium may cause cancer.
- Isotopes of thallium are used by doctors to find diseases in the body.

Lead
- In ancient times, lead was used in coins, sculpture, and pipes.
- Lead metal is used today in batteries, solder, and television screens.
- Compounds of lead were used in paint and gasoline, but because of the high toxicity, they are no longer used for these purposes.
- Oxides of lead are used to make decorative glass called crystal.
- Alloys of lead are used for printing type and as a radiation shield in nuclear power plants and X-ray machines.
- Isotopes of lead are used to determine the age of rocks.

Bismuth
- Compounds of bismuth are used to treat ulcers in the stomach and as a yellow pigment in cosmetics.
- Alloys of bismuth are used in fire alarms, fire sprinkler systems, and for casting and molding other metals.

Polonium
- Polonium is used in nuclear batteries for space equipment.
- Isotopes of polonium are used on dust-removal brushes and photographic film.

Astatine
- Astatine has no commercial uses.
- In lab experiments astatine is known to cause cancer in laboratory animals.
- Scientists believe astatine is taken up by the thyroid gland and may have a medical use in the future.

Chapter 2: Uses of Elements: *The Uses of the Elements Booklet*

Radon
- Radon gas is very toxic and can build up in homes. Radon detectors are suggested in homes where little or no fresh air gets in.
- Radon gas can cause lung cancer.
- Smoking a cigarette can be a source of harmful radon gas.
- Radon isotopes are used in cancer treatment.

Francium
- Francium has no known uses because of its high radioactivity and the small amounts of it that are available. It is estimated that less than an ounce of francium exists in the earth's crust.

Radium
- Radium was used in paint for watches to make the numbers glow in the dark until radiation was better understood.
- Radium is used to treat cancer.

Actinium
- Uses of actinium are impossible because it is radioactive and very rare.

Thorium
- Thorium has the potential to be a source of nuclear energy in the future.
- Thorium is used in camping lanterns.

Protactinium
- Protactinium has no known uses because it is radioactive and extremely rare.

Uranium
- In ancient times uranium was used to color glass and ceramics.
- Uranium is used as a fuel in nuclear reactors.
- Uranium isotopes are also used in glass for ceramics, weapons, and shielding against more dangerous radiation.

Neptunium
- Isotopes of neptunium are used in atomic bomb research, to make plutonium for atomic bombs, and were used as a power source for equipment on the moon.

Plutonium
- Isotopes are used in atomic bombs, nuclear reactors, and space exploration.

Americium
- Americium is used in smoke detectors.
- Isotopes of americium are used in nuclear reactors, airplane fuel gauges, and oil wells.

Curium
- Curium was used to analyze moon soils.
- Curium is used to power satellites.

Berkelium
- Berkelium has no uses because it is radioactive and decays very quickly.

Californium
- Californium isotopes are used to log oil wells.

Einsteinium
- Einsteinium has no uses because it is very radioactive and decays very quickly.

Fermium
- Fermium has no uses because it is radioactive and half will decay in less than a day.

Mendelevium
- Mendelevium has no uses because it is very radioactive and half will decay in 77 minutes.

Nobelium
- Nobelium has no uses because it is extremely radioactive and half will decay in less than an hour.

Chapter 2: Uses of Elements: *The Uses of the Elements Booklet*

Lawrencium
- There are no uses for lawrencium because it is extremely radioactive and half will decay in 30 seconds.

Rutherfordium
- There are no uses for rutherfordium because it is extremely radioactive and half will decay in 62 seconds.

Dubnium
- There are no uses for dubnium because it is extremely radioactive and half will decay in 34 seconds.

Seaborgium
- Seaborgium has no uses because it is extremely radioactive and half will decay in less than a second.

Bohrium
- Bohrium has no uses because it is extremely radioactive and almost nothing is known about it.

Hassium
- Hassium has no uses because it is extremely radioactive and almost nothing is known about this element.

Meitnerium
- Nothing is known about the properties of meitnerium. There are no uses.

Name: _____ Date: _____

Chapter 2: Uses of Elements: *Periodic Pictures*

Directions: Study each of the pictures below. Write the name of one element that is used for the object in each picture. Use the *Uses of the Elements* booklet to help you.

_____ 1.

_____ 2.

_____ 3.

_____ 4.

_____ 5.

_____ 6.

_____ 7.

_____ 8.

_____ 9.

_____ 10.

_____ 11.

_____ 12.

_____ 13.

_____ 14.

43

Name: _____   Date: _____

Chapter 2: Uses of Elements: *Places and Things*

Directions: List five elements that can be used in the following places and things. Use the *Uses of the Elements* booklet to help you.

A. Hospitals

    1. _____

    2. _____

    3. _____

    4. _____

    5. _____

B. Cameras

    1. _____

    2. _____

    3. _____

    4. _____

    5. _____

C. Nuclear Power Plants

    1. _____

    2. _____

    3. _____

    4. _____

    5. _____

D. Space Exploration

    1. _____

    2. _____

    3. _____

    4. _____

    5. _____

E. Batteries

    1. _____

    2. _____

    3. _____

    4. _____

    5. _____

F. Aircraft

    1. _____

    2. _____

    3. _____

    4. _____

    5. _____

G. Jewelry Store

    1. _____

    2. _____

    3. _____

    4. _____

    5. _____

H. Glass

    1. _____

    2. _____

    3. _____

    4. _____

    5. _____

I. Money

    1. _____

    2. _____

    3. _____

    4. _____

    5. _____

J. Home

    1. _____

    2. _____

    3. _____

    4. _____

    5. _____

Name: _____ Date: _____

Chapter 2: Uses of Elements: *Create a Table—Element Uses Group Work*

Purpose:
Most periodic tables that you see today contain the element name, symbol, atomic number, and a whole host of scientific data. The table that you will create in your group today will not have any scientific data. Instead, it will have drawings showing the uses of each element. Each group will be given a few elements to research and find uses for. You will draw pictures showing at least one use for each element you have been assigned. When the Create a Table is finished, you will have a poster-sized table showing how we use elements. The Create a Table will give you an idea of how the elements are used and how the periodic table is built.

Materials:
> Periodic cutouts, scissors, tape, colored pencils, *Uses of the Elements* booklet, Periodic Table

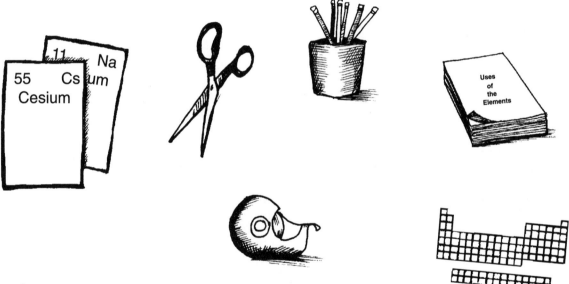

Procedures:
1. Get into your cooperative groups.
2. Obtain several periodic cutouts from your teacher.
3. Research the elements shown on your cutouts and find one or more uses that you would like to draw on your cutouts.
4. Make sure your cutouts are neat, clear, accurate, and colorful.
5. Cut out your elements and tape them together in the proper order with the cutouts that the other groups made for your periodic table.
6. Your class will end up with one wall-size periodic table showing at least one use for each element.

Chapter 2: Uses of Elements: *Create a Table —Element Uses Example Transparency Master*

6   C

Carbon

Chapter 2: Uses of Elements: *Create a Table Cutouts*

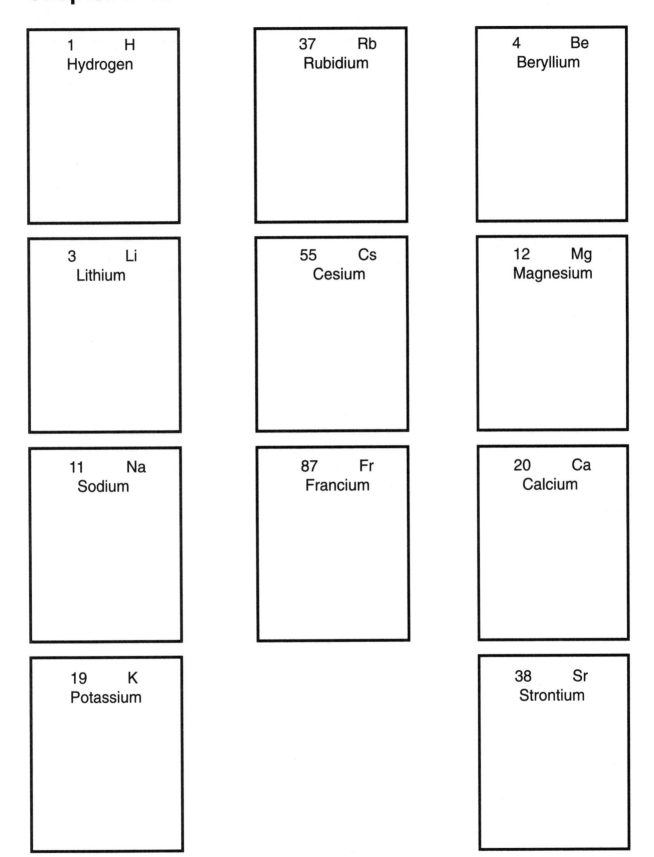

Chapter 2: Uses of Elements: *Create a Table Cutouts*

| 56   Ba |
| Barium |

| 21   Sc |
| Scandium |

| 22   Ti |
| Titanium |

| 88   Ra |
| Radium |

| 39   Y |
| Yttrium |

| 40   Zr |
| Zirconium |

| 57   La |
| Lanthanum |

| 72   Hf |
| Hafnium |

| 89   Ac |
| Actinium |

| 104   Rf |
| Rutherfordium |

Chapter 2: Uses of Elements: *Create a Table Cutouts*

23 V Vanadium	24 Cr Chromium	25 Mn Manganese
41 Nb Niobium	42 Mo Molybdenum	43 Tc Technetium
73 Ta Tantalum	74 W Tungsten	75 Re Rhenium
105 Db Dubnium	106 Sg Seaborgium	107 Bh Bohrium

Chapter 2: Uses of Elements: *Create a Table Cutouts*

26 Fe Iron	27 Co Cobalt	28 Ni Nickel
44 Ru Ruthenium	45 Rh Rhodium	46 Pd Palladium
76 Os Osmium	77 Ir Iridium	78 Pt Platinum
108 Hs Hassium	109 Mt Meitnerium	110 Uun Ununnilium

Chapter 2: Uses of Elements: *Create a Table Cutouts*

29 Cu Copper	30 Zn Zinc	5 B Boron
47 Ag Silver	48 Cd Cadmium	13 Al Aluminum
79 Au Gold	80 Hg Mercury	31 Ga Gallium
111 Uuu Unununium	112 Uub Ununbium	49 In Indium

Chapter 2: Uses of Elements: *Create a Table Cutouts*

6 C Carbon	7 N Nitrogen	81 Tl Thallium
14 Si Silicon	15 P Phosphorus	82 Pb Lead
32 Ge Germanium	33 As Arsenic	
50 Sn Tin	51 Sb Antimony	83 Bi Bismuth

52

Chapter 2: Uses of Elements: *Create a Table Cutouts*

8 O Oxygen	9 F Fluorine	84 Po Polonium

16 S Sulfur	17 Cl Chlorine	

34 Se Selenium	35 Br Bromine	

52 Te Tellurium	53 I Iodine	85 At Astatine

Chapter 2: Uses of Elements: *Create a Table Cutouts*

2   He Helium

54   Xe Xenon

10   Ne Neon

18   Ar Argon

36   Kr Krypton

86   Rn Radon

54

Chapter 2: Uses of Elements: *Create a Table Cutouts*

58 Ce Cerium	59 Pr Praseodymium	60 Nd Neodymium

90 Th Thorium	91 Pa Protactinium	92 U Uranium

61 Pm Promethium	62 Sm Samarium	63 Eu Europium

93 Np Neptunium	94 Pu Plutonium	95 Am Americium

55

Chapter 2: Uses of Elements: *Create a Table Cutouts*

64 Gd Gadolinium	65 Tb Terbium	66 Dy Dysprosium
96 Cm Curium	97 Bk Berkelium	98 Cf Californium
67 Ho Holmium	68 Er Erbium	69 Tm Thulium
99 Es Einsteinium	100 Fm Fermium	101 Md Mendelevium

Chapter 2: Uses of Elements: *Create a Table Cutouts*

70 Yb Ytterbium	71 Lu Lutetium
102 No Nobelium	103 Lr Lawrencium

Chapter 2: Uses of Elements: *Crossword Puzzle*

Name: _____   Date: _____

Directions: For each use below, place an element in the crossword puzzle. Use the *Uses of the Elements* booklet to help you.

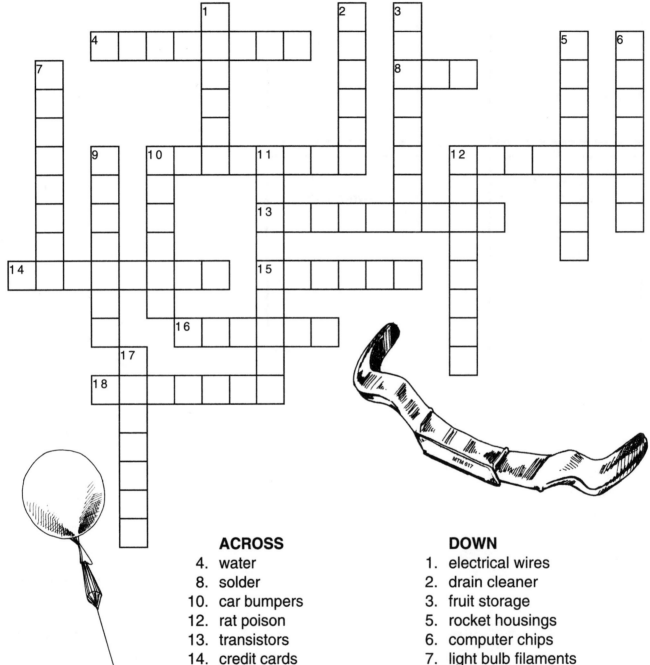

ACROSS
- 4. water
- 8. solder
- 10. car bumpers
- 12. rat poison
- 13. transistors
- 14. credit cards
- 15. pink glass
- 16. weather balloons
- 18. pacemakers

DOWN
- 1. electrical wires
- 2. drain cleaner
- 3. fruit storage
- 5. rocket housings
- 6. computer chips
- 7. light bulb filaments
- 9. bones and teeth
- 10. diamonds
- 11. heartburn relief
- 12. drink cans
- 17. overhead sprinklers

Name: _____ Date: _____

Chapter 2: Uses of Elements: *Review*

Directions: Study the *Uses of the Elements* booklet and answer the following questions.

Part I. Matching. Match the element to the use. Use each choice once.

	Uses		**Elements**
_____	1. Barometers	A.	Americium
_____	2. Bar code scanners	B.	Bismuth
_____	3. Blue glass	C.	Cerium
_____	4. Detects and causes bone diseases	D.	Cobalt
_____	5. Dynamite	E.	Fluorine
_____	6. Heating element in toasters	F.	Helium
_____	7. Makes toys glow	G.	Iodine
_____	8. Polishes camera lenses	H.	Mercury
_____	9. Possible future nuclear fuel	I.	Neodymium
_____	10. Purifies water	J.	Nickel
_____	11. Razor blades	K.	Nitrogen
_____	12. Smoke detectors	L.	Phosphorus
_____	13. Non-stick coating	M.	Platinum
_____	14. Tells if paper money is counterfeit	N.	Strontium
_____	15. Treats stomach ulcers	O.	Thorium

Part II. Element Uses. Write at least one use for each of the following elements.

16. Aluminum _____

17. Lanthanum _____

18. Iron _____

19. Oxygen _____

20. Carbon _____

21. Gold _____

22. Lead _____

23. Copper _____

24. Silicon _____

25. Chlorine _____

Name: _____ Date: _____

Chapter 2: Uses of Elements: *Quiz*

Part I. Harlan's Day. Carefully read the story below. On the next page, list ten elements that Harlan used that day and justify your answer. Study the example, but do not use boron in your answer.

Harlan's Day

When Harlan woke up on that cold January morning, the first thing he did was look out the window of his bedroom at the thermometer. Then he went into the bathroom to take a shower, shampoo his hair with dandruff shampoo, and brush his teeth. He went downstairs to make a couple pieces of toast with margarine on them. He kept the bread in the toaster too long and it set off the smoke detector. When the smoke cleared, he then asked his mother for lunch money. He also needed money because it was picture day at school. He then gathered his books and put on his coat and made his way to the bus stop.

Harlan's first class was social studies. There he learned that the police got the name "cop" because they used to wear copper buttons. Second hour, Harlan went to math. He forgot his calculator that day, so he borrowed one from his teacher, Ms. Posley. She gave him a detention for that. Third hour was gym. As soon as Harlan put his gym clothes on, the fire alarm rang. Harlan had to go outside on that cold January day wearing only his gym clothes. By the time fourth hour rolled around, Harlan was in tech. ed. It was his day to operate the robotics arm with a computer. It was cool. He programmed the arm to pick up a credit card in only 43 moves. After tech. ed., Harlan went to lunch. There he got yelled at by Mr. Burke, the assistant principal, because he didn't put his soda can in the recycling bin. Harlan asked Mr. Burke if he knew who pulled the fire alarm. Mr. Burke told Harlan it was none of his business.

Fifth hour Harlan went to band. There he was the star of the brass section. He was the first chair trumpet player. The band practiced several songs from the movie *Grease*. Sixth hour was English. The class went to the auditorium to get their pictures taken. Seventh hour was science, his favorite subject. There they did a cool experiment using beakers and test tubes. After the experiment, he learned how cancer is treated using radiation. Harlan went to his after-school detention for forgetting his calculator. There he worked on his science report on brain disorders.

When Harlan got home from school that day, he relaxed by playing with his remote-controlled car in his driveway. What a day!

Name: _____ Date: _____

Chapter 2: Uses of Elements: *Quiz*

Elements	Justification
Example: *Boron*	*Used in calculators. Harlan forgot his that day.*

1. _____   _____

2. _____   _____

3. _____   _____

4. _____   _____

5. _____   _____

6. _____   _____

7. _____   _____

8. _____   _____

9. _____   _____

10. _____   _____

Part II. You Make the Comic Strip. In the three frames below, make a comic strip that shows how at least one element is used. Make sure that your drawings are neat and clear. Use captions on each frame to help tell your story.

_____

Title of Your Comic

Chapter 3: Element Symbols: *The Teacher's Guide*

Page 64 - Element Symbols You Should Know

Students are given rules for writing one-letter element symbols, two-letter element symbols, and three-letter symbols. At the bottom of this activity, students are asked to correctly write the symbols for 25 elements using a periodic table. These 25 elements were selected because they are commonly used in many areas of science. The students are asked to memorize these 25 symbols.

Page 65 - Symbols to Know

In this activity students will practice memorizing the symbols of the 25 elements mentioned on page 64. Students will also practice using the periodic table by finding some atomic numbers and by finding the state of matter for all the elements. Students may want to use colored pencils on periodic table B; however, this can be done in black and white.

Pages 67-69 - Element Symbols Cards

In this group activity the students should fill in the elements and symbols cards that are missing on page 68. The students should then take the elements and symbols from page 64, and write them in the proper spaces on page 67. At this point, they will cut out all the cards and tape the symbols together with the proper element. They are best assembled on a colored sheet of legal paper. If colored legal paper is not available, then any sheet will do, including notebook paper. Reproduce enough element symbols practice sheets, page 67, for every student in the class. Make enough element symbols and cards sheets, page 68, for each group. A grading rubric has been provided on page 69 if the teacher desires to use this. In this activity the students are also required to make flash cards for the elements and symbols. Students can use the flash cards to practice memorizing the symbols and elements. The symbols and elements in this activity are the same ones mentioned on page 64.

Page 70 - Element Symbols Create a Phrase

Here students can create words, phrases, or sentences using any of the element symbols on the periodic table. Examples are given at the top of the activity sheet. It is fun at the completion of this activity to have students volunteer their best answer and see what words, phrases, and sentences they came up with.

Chapter 3: Element Symbols: *The Teacher's Guide (cont.)*

<u>Page 71 - Names and Symbols Do Not Match</u>

In this chapter, students will notice that some of the element names and symbols do not match. For example, silver's symbol is Ag. Students should be taught that these elements have names in other languages and that those languages were used to make the symbols. In this activity, students are asked to match the English name with the foreign name. This is easily done by looking at the symbols for each of the elements listed. The students are also asked to create English symbols for the elements with foreign symbols. When this activity is completed, it is suggested that teachers call on volunteers in the class to offer their created symbols.

<u>Page 72–74 - Symbols Practice Quizzes I–III</u>

A variety of practice quizzes are provided for memorizing the 25 elements mentioned on page 64. These quizzes are best used as gathering activities at the beginning of the period. It is recommended that students not be allowed to use their notes, books, portfolios, or periodic tables. These quizzes are fast and easily checked. They are designed to give students a chance to see what elements and symbols they need to practice.

<u>Pages 75–76 - Element Symbols Test</u>

This test is designed to see what elements and symbols the students have memorized from the list on page 64. The test consists of three parts. In Part I, students need to write the symbol for the element mentioned in the sentence. In Part II, students will identify the elements written in the molecular formulas. In Part III, students will write the name of the element mentioned in a sentence that uses the element symbol.

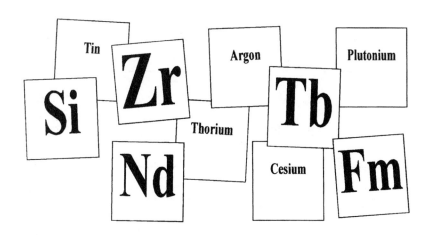

Name: _____ Date: _____

Chapter 3: Element Symbols: *Element Symbols You Should Know*

Every Element Has a Symbol. All the elements have symbols. The symbols are used as a kind of shorthand for writing chemical formulas and equations. Many scientists only write the symbols and never write the true name of the element. The system used for making the symbols is as follows.

One-Letter Symbols. Fourteen (14) elements on the periodic table have one-letter symbols. The one-letter symbols are always capitalized.
Example: The symbol for carbon is **C**.

Two-Letter Symbols. Ninety-five (95) elements have two-letter symbols. In these elements the first letter is always capitalized and the second letter is always in the lower case.
Example: The symbol for neon is **Ne**.

Three-Letter Symbols. The last three (3) elements in this periodic table have three-letter symbols. The first letter is always capitalized and the last two are in the lower case. These are all new elements and have not yet been officially named. New elements are given Latin names that correspond to their atomic numbers. Some periodic tables today list elements up to #118.
Example: The symbol for ununbium is **Uub**.

Directions: Look up each of the following elements in your periodic table and correctly write the symbol in the space provided. These elements are elements you should know. Have your teacher check to see if you have correctly written each symbol, then memorize each symbol for each element.

1. Aluminum _____   10. Iron _____   18. Potassium _____
2. Calcium _____   11. Lead _____   19. Silicon _____
3. Carbon _____   12. Magnesium _____   20. Silver _____
4. Chlorine _____   13. Mercury _____   21. Sodium _____
5. Copper _____   14. Nickel _____   22. Sulfur _____
6. Gold _____   15. Nitrogen _____   23. Tin _____
7. Helium _____   16. Oxygen _____   24. Uranium _____
8. Hydrogen _____   17. Phosphorus _____   25. Zinc _____
9. Iodine _____

Name: _____ Date: _____

Chapter 3: Element Symbols: *Symbols to Know*

Purpose: To become familiar with the periodic table. To practice memorizing 25 symbols.

Procedure:

1. Find all 25 elements below in the periodic table and place them in the proper place in <u>Periodic Table A</u> on page 66. Only write the symbols in the table.

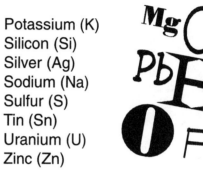

Aluminum (Al)	Iron (Fe)	Potassium (K)
Calcium (Ca)	Lead (Pb)	Silicon (Si)
Carbon (C)	Magnesium (Mg)	Silver (Ag)
Chlorine (Cl)	Mercury (Hg)	Sodium (Na)
Copper (Cu)	Nickel (Ni)	Sulfur (S)
Gold (Au)	Nitrogen (N)	Tin (Sn)
Helium (He)	Oxygen (O)	Uranium (U)
Hydrogen (H)	Phosphorus (P)	Zinc (Zn)
Iodine (I)		

2. Indicate the state of matter (solid, liquid, or gas) of each element in <u>Periodic Table B</u> on page 66. Please show a legend for the colors and symbols that you use.

3. Use your periodic table to complete the table below.

Element	Symbol	Atomic Number
Chromium		
Titanium		
Beryllium		
Strontium		
Arsenic		
Neon		
Argon		
Fluorine		
Cobalt		
Lithium		

Name: _____ Date: _____

Chapter 3: Element Symbols: *Symbols to Know (cont.)*

Periodic Table A

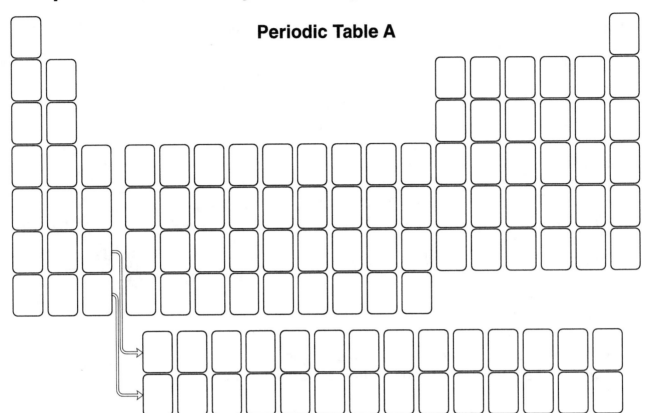

Periodic Table B

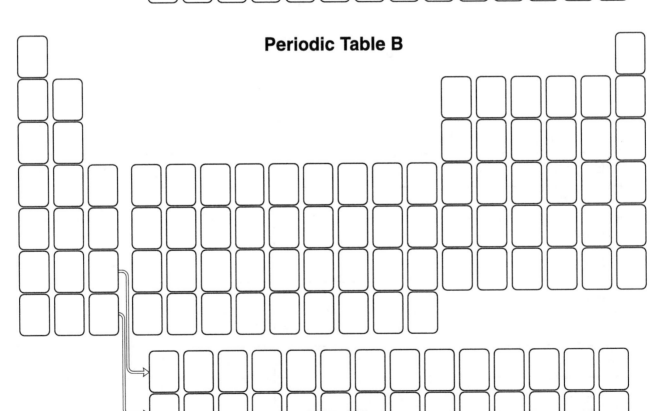

Name: _____ Date: _____

Chapter 3: Element Symbols: *Element Symbols Practice*

1. All 25 elements and symbols should be listed on page 68, but some are missing. Use the worksheets *Element Symbols You Should Know* and *Elements and Symbols Cards* to complete the following lists.

Symbols Present	Elements Present	Symbols Missing	Elements Missing
_____	_____	_____	_____
_____	_____	_____	_____
_____	_____	_____	_____
_____	_____	_____	_____
_____	_____	_____	_____
_____	_____	_____	_____
_____	_____	_____	_____
_____	_____	_____	
_____	_____		
_____	_____		
_____	_____		
_____	_____		
_____	_____		
_____	_____		
_____	_____		
_____	_____		
_____			

Materials:
Elements and Symbols Cards
Element Symbols You Should Know
Scissors
Tape
Colored Paper
25 - 3″ x 5″ Index Cards

2. Fill in the blank cards with the missing elements and symbols.
3. Use scissors to cut out each card.
4. Match the elements to the symbols and tape the matching cards together on a colored sheet of paper.
5. Use your cards to test each other on the elements and symbols.
6. Make flash cards. Use 25 - 3″ x 5″ index cards to make your flash cards. Write each element on one side and the corresponding symbol on the back.
7. Test each other using the flash cards and the elements symbols cards.

Chapter 3: Element Symbols: *Elements and Symbols Cards*

Hydrogen	Cu	K	Potassium	Lead
Fe	Chlorine	Phosphorus	He	Hg
Silicon	N	Magnesium	Calcium	Na
Mercury	Al	H	Silver	C
Au	Aluminum	U	S	Nitrogen
Ni	Sulfur	Zinc	Tin	O
Ag	P	Iodine	Gold	Pb

Chapter 3: Element Symbols: *Element Symbols Cards Rubric*

Symbols Cards (5 points)

5   Excellent! The cards are taped neatly on the colored paper. The symbols and names are in neat rows and columns. The printing is neat. The cards have been taped together accurately. The cards are easy to use.

4   Good! The cards look good on the colored paper. The printing is neat and accurate. The cards are easy to use.

3   Unsatisfactory! The symbols and names are not matched up correctly. The printing may not be neat or accurate. The cards are difficult to use.

0–2   Poor! Sloppy! Taped and cut quickly just to get done. The cards are not usable.

Total symbol cards points out of 5   _____

Symbols Sheet (5 points)

5   Excellent! No blank spaces on the list. Elements and symbols have all been identified correctly and are properly noted on the worksheet.

4   Good! No blank spaces on the list. All of the elements and symbols have been identified.

3   Unsatisfactory! Blank spaces appear on the lists. Elements and symbols are not identified or are misidentified.

0–2   Poor! Sloppy! Lists are sloppily done in order to get finished quickly.

Total symbols sheet points out of 5   _____

Flash Cards (5 points)

5   Excellent! Flash cards are well done and easy to use.

4   Good! Flash cards look good and are easy to use.

3   Average! Flash cards are usable.

0–2   Poor! Flash cards are unusable.

Total flash card points out of 5   _____

Social Skills (5 points)

5   Excellent! Everybody participated. Group attended well to the teacher. Students used quiet voices and only worked with the members of the group. Students stayed on task. Students finished the activities in the given amount of time.

4   Good! Students did a good job of following the above social skills.

3   Unsatisfactory! Students worked efficiently but from time to time violated one or more of the social skills.

0–2   Poor! Work was seriously impeded by frequent violations of the above social skills.

Total social skills points out of 5   _____

Total points out of 20   _____

Percent out of 100   _____

Final Group Grade on Elements Cards   A B C D F

Name: _____ Date: _____

Chapter 3: Element Symbols: *Create a Phrase*

Directions: Create a word, phrase, or sentence using element symbols. Try to use the 25 elements that you need to memorize; however, you may use any symbol on the periodic table. Good luck.

Examples:

Word: Snag (Sn = Tin and Ag = Silver)

Phrase: Sun's Up (S = Sulfur, U = Uranium, N = Nitrogen, S = Sulfur, U = Uranium, and P = Phosphorus)

Sentence: Al Hopkins is in Ohio. (Al = Aluminum, H = Hydrogen, O = Oxygen, P = Phosphorus, K = Potassium, I = Iodine, N = Nitrogen, S = Sulfur, I = Iodine, S = Sulfur, I = Iodine, N = Nitrogen, O = Oxygen, H = Hydrogen, I = Iodine, and O = Oxygen)

1. _____

2. _____

3. _____

4. _____

5. _____

6. _____

7. _____

8. _____

9. _____

10. _____

11. _____

12. _____

13. _____

14. _____

15. _____

Name: _____ Date: _____

Chapter 3: Element Symbols: *Names and Symbols Do Not Match*

Directions: You've probably noticed that some of the names of the elements do not match the symbols. That's because some symbols are made from the Latin or German name of the element. Let's test your ability to identify the element by the foreign name. Look up the symbol on your periodic table and see if you can match the English name to the Latin or German name. Use each letter once.

English	Latin or German
_____ 1. Antimony	A. Argentum
_____ 2. Copper	B. Aurum
_____ 3. Gold	C. Cuprum
_____ 4. Iron	D. Ferrum
_____ 5. Lead	E. Hydrargyrum
_____ 6. Mercury	F. Kaium
_____ 7. Potassium	G. Natrium
_____ 8. Silver	H. Plumbum
_____ 9. Sodium	I. Stannum
_____ 10. Tin	J. Stibium
_____ 11. Tungsten	K. Wolfran

Directions: All of the following elements have English names and foreign symbols. Assign each of them a symbol based on their English names. Be sure to use one or two letters, and that the English symbol doesn't already exist.

12. Sodium	_____	18. Antimony	_____
13. Potassium	_____	19. Tungsten	_____
14. Iron	_____	20. Gold	_____
15. Copper	_____	21. Mercury	_____
16. Silver	_____	22. Lead	_____
17. Tin	_____		

71

Name: _____ Date: _____

Chapter 3: Element Symbols: *Symbols Practice Quiz I*

Fold the page in half lengthwise before completing each column.

Directions: Write the symbol in the space.   **Directions:** Write the name in the space.

1.	Magnesium	_____	26.	Ag	_____
2.	Gold	_____	27.	Al	_____
3.	Hydrogen	_____	28.	Au	_____
4.	Carbon	_____	29.	C	_____
5.	Oxygen	_____	30.	Ca	_____
6.	Sulfur	_____	31.	Cl	_____
7.	Silicon	_____	32.	Cu	_____
8.	Copper	_____	33.	Fe	_____
9.	Sodium	_____	34.	H	_____
10.	Nickel	_____	35.	He	_____
11.	Aluminum	_____	36.	Hg	_____
12.	Zinc	_____	37.	I	_____
13.	Uranium	_____	38.	K	_____
14.	Iodine	_____	39.	Mg	_____
15.	Phosphorus	_____	40.	N	_____
16.	Chlorine	_____	41.	Na	_____
17.	Calcium	_____	42.	Ni	_____
18.	Iron	_____	43.	O	_____
19.	Helium	_____	44.	P	_____
20.	Tin	_____	45.	Pb	_____
21.	Silver	_____	46.	S	_____
22.	Mercury	_____	47.	Si	_____
23.	Potassium	_____	48.	Sn	_____
24.	Nitrogen	_____	49.	U	_____
25.	Lead	_____	50.	Zn	_____

Name: _____ Date: _____

Chapter 3: Element Symbols: *Symbols Practice Quiz II*

Directions: Below is a list of elements and symbols. Complete the list correctly and you ace the quiz.

	Name	**Symbol**
1.	Nickel	_____
2.	_____	N
3.	_____	Hg
4.	Iron	_____
5.	Silver	_____
6.	Potassium	_____
7.	_____	S
8.	_____	Si
9.	_____	Sn
10.	Gold	_____
11.	Aluminum	_____
12.	_____	Ca
13.	_____	C
14.	_____	Cl
15.	_____	Cu
16.	Sodium	_____
17.	Helium	_____
18.	Hydrogen	_____
19.	_____	Pb
20.	_____	Mg
21.	_____	O
22.	Phosphorus	_____
23.	Zinc	_____
24.	Iodine	_____
25.	Uranium	_____

Name: _____ Date: _____

Chapter 3: Element Symbols: *Symbols Practice Quiz III*

Directions: Match the element to the symbol. Use each of the choices once. Write the letter of the symbol on the blank.

	Element		Symbol
_____ 1.	Hydrogen	A.	Ag
_____ 2.	Helium	B.	Al
_____ 3.	Carbon	C.	Au
_____ 4.	Nitrogen	D.	C
_____ 5.	Oxygen	E.	Ca
_____ 6.	Sodium	F.	Cl
_____ 7.	Magnesium	G.	Cu
_____ 8.	Iron	H.	Fe
_____ 9.	Nickel	I.	H
_____ 10.	Copper	J.	He
_____ 11.	Zinc	K.	Hg
_____ 12.	Potassium	L.	I
_____ 13.	Calcium	M.	K
_____ 14	Aluminum	N.	Mg
_____ 15.	Silicon	O.	N
_____ 16.	Phosphorus	P.	Na
_____ 17.	Sulfur	Q.	Ni
_____ 18.	Chlorine	R.	O
_____ 19.	Iodine	S.	P
_____ 20.	Silver	T.	Pb
_____ 21.	Gold	U.	S
_____ 22.	Mercury	V.	Si
_____ 23.	Lead	W.	Sn
_____ 24.	Uranium	X.	U
_____ 25.	Tin	Y.	Zn

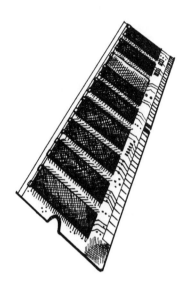

Name: _____ Date: _____

Chapter 3: Element Symbols: *Test*

Part I. Sentences: Write the symbol of the element mentioned in each sentence.

1. Mercury is used in some thermometers.   _____

2. Uranium provides us with fuel for nuclear power.   _____

3. Bones and teeth are made mostly of calcium.   _____

4. Diamonds are made of carbon.   _____

5. Some balloons are filled with helium.   _____

6. We get the oxygen that we breathe from the air.   _____

7. Germs get killed by chlorine in swimming pools.   _____

8. Our air is 78 percent nitrogen.   _____

9. Magnesium is found in some heartburn medicine.   _____

10. Amethyst jewelry is made of silicon.   _____

11. Bananas are a source of potassium for the body.   _____

12. Sulfur is the main ingredient in gunpowder.   _____

13. Pennies are coated with copper.   _____

14. Tin is used to make foil and cans.   _____

15. A healthy thyroid gland needs iodine.   _____

16. Lead is a heavy metal that is toxic to humans.   _____

17. Gold is one of a few elements that is found in its pure form.   _____

18. Silver can be used to make mirrors.   _____

19. Zinc is used to coat many objects made of steel.   _____

20. Sodium can be found in salt.   _____

21. Magnets are made mostly of iron.   _____

22. Phosphorus is used to make objects glow.   _____

23. Hydrogen is the lightest element that we have.   _____

24. Aluminum is a light metal used in planes.   _____

25. Nickel makes up 25 percent of a U.S. five-cent piece.   _____

75

Name: _____ Date: _____

Chapter 3: Element Symbols: *Test*

Part II. Formulas: Below is a list of the chemical formulas of many common compounds. Write the name of the underlined symbol in each formula in the space provided.

26. Water: H$_2$$\underline{O}$ _____

27. Salt: $\underline{Na}$Cl _____

28. Sulfuric Acid: $\underline{H}_2$SO$_4$ _____

29. Quartz: $\underline{Si}$O$_2$ _____

30. Rust: $\underline{Fe}_2$O$_3$ _____

31. Baking Soda: NaH$\underline{C}$O$_3$ _____

32. Photo Developer: $\underline{Ag}$Cl _____

33. Ammonia: $\underline{N}$H$_3$ _____

34. Fool's Gold: Fe$\underline{S}_2$ _____

35. Stomach Acid: H$\underline{Cl}$ _____

Part III. Symbols: Symbols of elements are used in the sentences below. Write the name of the element for the symbol used in the sentence in the space provided.

36. I is used by campers to purify water. _____

37. Mg is used to treat skin rashes. _____

38. Some switches contain Hg. _____

39. Some glass plates are coated with Au. _____

40. Some pots and pans are made of Al. _____

41. Wire made of Ni is used in toasters. _____

42. Some bowls and plates are made of Sn. _____

43. Pb is used to make television screens. _____

44. P is used by the body. _____

45. Some liquid soaps use K. _____

46. Cu is used for paint on ships. _____

47. Zn is used to make brass. _____

48. Ca is used in building materials. _____

49. He is used in bar code scanners. _____

50. Some weapons are made from U. _____

Chapter 4: Organization of the Periodic Table: *The Teacher's Guide*

Pages 79-81 - Organizing the Elements Brochure

This brochure will give the students a brief orientation as to how the periodic table is organized. It may be read either by volunteers in class, or each student can read it silently. This brochure can be reproduced for every student in the class, or classroom sets can be made. Each entry in the brochure should be discussed.

Pages 82-83 - Study Guide to the Periodic Table Brochure

This study guide is designed to be used with the brochure on pages 79-81. It can be done individually in class or as homework. Students will need the brochure and a periodic table to complete the activity. This activity is easily graded by the teacher or can be graded in class by having the students trade papers and the teacher read the answers.

Pages 84-86 - Why Are Elements Put Into Families?

In this laboratory, students will test three salts of alkali metals and three salts of alkaline earth metals on how they react with ammonium compounds. The alkaline earth metals will form a precipitate and the alkali metals will not. This laboratory is designed to demonstrate how different families react differently to the same reagents. This lab is best done in cooperative groups. However, it's best to make copies for each student.

Pages 87-88 - The Scientific Method - Why Are Elements Put Into Families? - Laboratory Quiz

Use this quiz as a follow-up to the laboratory on pages 84-86. If the students have been exposed to the scientific method, this is a great way to tie in the periodic table and the scientific method. If they have not been exposed to the scientific method, the teacher may want to do a mini scientific method unit. This lab is flexible enough to be done in cooperative groups or individually. If this quiz is done in groups, only make enough copies for each group. If this quiz is done individually, then teachers will have to make enough copies for each student.

Pages 89-91 - Families of Elements Poster Activity

In this group activity, teachers should assign each cooperative group a family of elements to research and design a poster that teaches the characteristics, examples, uses, and drawings of that family. Page 89 provides the directions and a place to draw a rough draft of the poster. Pages 90 and 91 provide a grading rubric for the finished poster if the teacher chooses to grade the poster in this way.

Chapter 4: Organization of the Periodic Table: *The Teacher's Guide (cont.)*

Pages 92-96 - The Families of Elements Resource Information

These pages provide a basic resource that students can use to research their element family for the activity on page 89. Other resources should be made available to the students for the activity on page 89. Resources such as textbooks, encyclopedias, interactive periodic table for computers, periodic table, and the *Uses of the Elements* booklet (pages 32-42) can be used for this activity.

Pages 97-98 - Families of Elements Group Quiz

Teachers should make enough quizzes for each group. After the element families posters that were designed on page 89 have been posted around the room, the groups will be able to find most of their answers on the posters. Allow the groups to walk around the room to view the posters. The groups should also have resources available to look up any answers they can't find on the posters.

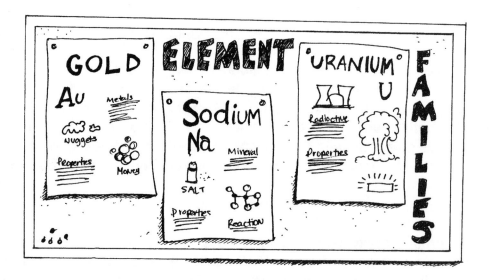

Chapter 4: Organization of the Periodic Table: *Organizing the Elements Brochure*

The Periodic Table of the Elements

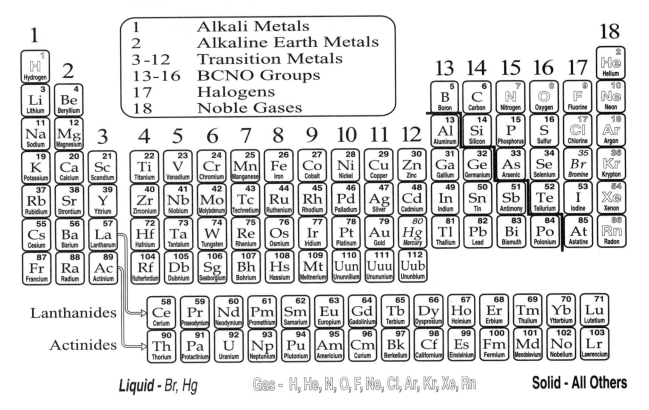

1	Alkali Metals
2	Alkaline Earth Metals
3-12	Transition Metals
13-16	BCNO Groups
17	Halogens
18	Noble Gases

Liquid - *Br, Hg*   Gas - H, He, N, O, F, Ne, Cl, Ar, Kr, Xe, Rn   **Solid - All Others**

A Way of Organizing the Elements

Introduction

In 1869, a Russian scientist by the name of Dimitry Mendeleyev constructed the first periodic table. Mendeleyev wanted to organize the elements according to their properties. His periodic table looked very much like the one that we use today. Today's periodic table not only organizes the elements by their properties, but it allows us to tell much about an element by its position on the table.

Most periodic tables today tell the element's name, symbol, atomic number, family, and give a whole host of scientific information like atomic mass and electron configuration. Even though different periodic tables may show the information differently, they usually contain a key that tells us how to find the information we need. Many times you will see a key like this:

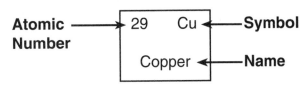

Atomic Number ⟶ 29   Cu ⟵ Symbol

Copper ⟵ Name

79

Chapter 4: Organization of the Periodic Table: *Organizing the Elements Brochure*

Atomic Number

Every element has an atomic number. This is the number of protons in its atom. A proton is a positively-charged particle in an atom. For example, the element copper has 29 protons in its atom. If you read the periodic table left to right and row by row, the atomic numbers will increase in order until you get to number 57. This is because elements 58-71 and 90-103 appear in order in the two rows at the bottom of the periodic table, which are called the lanthanides and actinides.

Symbols

Each element is assigned a symbol. The symbol usually corresponds to the element's name. Symbols are usually two letters. However, some symbols have one or three letters.

Families

Each vertical column on the periodic table is an element family. All of the elements in each family have similar properties. They usually react the same in chemical reactions, and they may even look the same and be used for the same purposes. Each family is numbered and has a name. Most periodic tables show the number; some will even give the name.

Periods

Each horizontal row is called a period. There are seven periods on the periodic table. The lanthanides and actinides really fit in with the sixth and seventh periods. They have been written at the bottom of the table for convenience.

Metals, Nonmetals, and Metalloids

Some periodic tables show a bold line in the shape of steps on the right side of the periodic table. All the elements to the left of that line are metals. You can probably see that most of the elements are metals. Metals are elements that are good conductors of heat and electricity. They have a shiny, metallic luster. Metals can also be pounded into shapes or drawn into wire.

All of the elements to the right of the bold step-shaped line are called nonmetals. Nonmetals are poor conductors of heat and electricity. They usually have a dull or earthy luster. When pounded, nonmetals usually shatter or form powders.

The elements that touch the bold step-shaped line are called metalloids. These elements have characteristics of both metals and nonmetals.

Chapter 4: Organization of the Periodic Table: *Organizing the Elements Brochure*

Solid, Liquid, or Gas

Some periodic tables even tell us whether an element is a solid, liquid, or gas at room temperature. This is sometimes done by color or by the type of print used. Most elements are solids. There are a few gases. Only mercury and bromine are liquids at room temperature. All elements can be solids, liquids, and gases; it simply depends on the temperature.

Radioactivity

Some elements are radioactive and do not have a stable form. Radioactive means that they naturally give off particles. All the elements with an atomic number of 84 or greater are radioactive. Technetium (43) and promethium (61) also have no stable form. All elements have radioactive forms, and most elements have stable forms. Some periodic tables show whether an element is radioactive or stable.

Natural or Manmade

Most of the elements that we see on the periodic table are natural. This means that they occur somewhere in nature. These are called the natural elements. Synthetic elements are elements that are made by humans in laboratories. Many of the heavier elements are synthetic. It was once thought that neptunium (93) and plutonium (94) were synthetic, but now they have been found in small amounts in nature. All of the elements with an atomic number of 95 or greater are synthetic. Some periodic tables show whether an element is natural or synthetic.

Name: _____ Date: _____

Chapter 4: Organization of the Periodic Table: *Study Guide to the Organizing the Elements Brochure*

Directions: Read and study the *Organizing the Elements* brochure. Use the brochure and the periodic table to answer the questions below.

Part I. Vocabulary You Should Know: The following is a list of vocabulary words from the brochure that you should know. Match the word to its definition. Use each choice once.

_____ 1. Each horizontal row in the periodic table

_____ 2. Each vertical column in the periodic table

_____ 3. Elements that give off particles

_____ 4. Elements that are made in laboratories

_____ 5. Elements that occur somewhere on earth

_____ 6. Elements that are good conductors of heat and electricity. They can be pounded into shapes or drawn into wires. They have a shiny, metallic luster. They appear on the periodic table to the left of the bold step-shaped line.

_____ 7. Elements that are poor conductors of heat and electricity. If pounded, they will shatter or get crushed to a powder. They have a dull or earthy luster. They appear to the right of the bold step-shaped line in the periodic table.

_____ 8. Elements that have characteristics of both metals and nonmetals. They touch the bold step-shaped line in the periodic table.

_____ 9. The number of protons in an atom of an element. The elements are put in this order.

_____ 10. Organizes the elements by their properties

A. Atomic Number

B. Family

C. Metalloids

D. Metals

E. Natural

F. Nonmetals

G. Period

H. Periodic table

I. Radioactive

J. Synthetic

Name: _____ Date: _____

Chapter 4: Organization of the Periodic Table: *Study Guide to the Organizing the Elements Brochure*

Part II. Gathering Information From the Periodic Table: Give the following information about each of the elements listed below. Use a copy of the periodic table on page 15.

Copper

11. Atomic Number   _____
12. Symbol   _____
13. Family Number   _____
14. Family Name   _____
15. Solid, Liquid, or Gas _____
16. Metal, Nonmetal, or Metalloid _____
17. Natural or Manmade   _____
18. Radioactive or Stable _____

Calcium

35. Atomic Number   _____
36. Symbol   _____
37. Family Number   _____
38. Family Name   _____
39. Solid, Liquid, or Gas _____
40. Metal, Nonmetal, or Metalloid _____
41. Natural or Manmade   _____
42. Radioactive or Stable _____

Mercury

19. Atomic Number   _____
20. Symbol   _____
21. Family Number   _____
22. Family Name   _____
23. Solid, Liquid, or Gas _____
24. Metal, Nonmetal, or Metalloid _____
25. Natural or Manmade   _____
26. Radioactive or Stable _____

Uranium

43. Atomic Number   _____
44. Symbol   _____
45. Family Number   _____
46. Family Name   _____
47. Solid, Liquid, or Gas _____
48. Metal, Nonmetal, or Metalloid _____
49. Natural or Manmade   _____
50. Radioactive or Stable _____

Oxygen

27. Atomic Number   _____
28. Symbol   _____
29. Family Number   _____
30. Family Name   _____
31. Solid, Liquid, or Gas _____
32. Metal, Nonmetal, or Metalloid _____
33. Natural or Manmade   _____
34. Radioactive or Stable _____

O_2

Name: _____ Date: _____

Chapter 4: Organization of the Periodic Table: *Why Are Elements Put Into Families?*

Purpose: To experiment with salts of the alkali metals and the alkaline earth metals. To test two of the families on the periodic table to see how they react with ammonium compounds. To understand why scientists put elements into families.

Materials:

Safety Materials
Safety goggles
Apron

Chemicals (0.5M solutions)
Ammonium carbonate
Ammonium phosphate
Barium chloride
Calcium chloride
Lithium chloride
Potassium chloride
Sodium chloride
Strontium chloride

Laboratory Equipment
Six test tubes
Test tube rack
Eight Barnes bottles
(Any bottles with
eyedroppers will do)
Distilled water

Procedures

1. Put on the safety goggles and the aprons.

2. Label the test tubes A, B, C, D, E, and F. Place them in order in the test tube rack.

3. Notice that each Barnes bottle is labeled with the letters A-F. Place each Barnes bottle in front of the corresponding test tube. (The two extra bottles hold the ammonium carbonate and phosphate.)

4. Add five drops from each Barnes bottle to the corresponding test tube, so five drops of chemical A are in test tube A, five drops of chemical B are in test tube B, and so on to F.

5. Add three drops of ammonium carbonate to each test tube.

6. Observe the test tubes for a couple of minutes. If a milky substance appears in the test tube, then a precipitate has formed. Indicate with a P on Table 1 for the chemicals that formed a precipitate. If a milky substance did not form, then a precipitate did not form. Indicate with an NP on Table 1 for the chemicals that did not form a precipitate.

7. Empty, rinse, and clean the substances from the test tubes with distilled water.

8. Repeat the experiment, but instead of adding ammonium carbonate, add ammonium phosphate this time.

Name: _____ Date: _____

Chapter 4: Organization of the Periodic Table: *Why Are Elements Put Into Families?*

Observations:

Table 1

Letter	Chemicals	Reaction With Ammonium Carbonate (P or NP)	Reaction With Ammonium Phosphate (P or NP)
A	Barium Chloride		
B	Calcium Chloride		
C	Lithium Chloride		
D	Potassium Chloride		
E	Sodium Chloride		
F	Strontium Chloride		

Conclusions:

1. What conclusions can you draw from this experiment based on the way the elements are put into the periodic table?

    _____

    _____

    _____

    _____

2. List two examples from the element families represented in this experiment.

    _____

    _____

    _____

3. How did the alkali metal compounds react to the ammonium compounds?

    _____

    _____

    _____

Name: _____ Date: _____

Chapter 4: Organization of the Periodic Table: *Why Are Elements Put Into Families?*

4. How did the alkaline earth metals react to the ammonium compounds?

_____

_____

_____

5. Fill in Table 2 by predicting how the elements in the table would react to the ammonium compounds.

Table 2

Element	Reaction with Ammonium Carbonate (P or NP)	Reaction with Ammonium Phosphate (P or NP)
Beryllium		
Cesium		
Francium		
Magnesium		
Radium		
Rubidium		

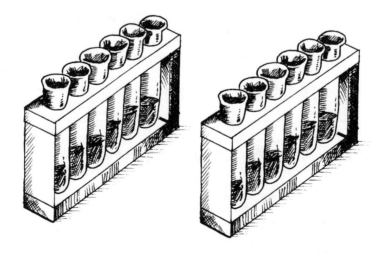

Name: _____   Date: _____

Chapter 4: Organization of the Periodic Table: *The Scientific Method—Why Are Elements Put Into Families?*

Laboratory Quiz

Directions: Use your lab sheet and your periodic table to answer the following questions about the experiment you performed. Write clearly written, complete answers for each of the following questions.

1. Write a problem that would fit this experiment.

    _____

    _____

    _____

2. Write a hypothesis that would fit this experiment.

    _____

    _____

    _____

3. List the materials and chemicals that you used to perform this experiment.

    _____

    _____

    _____

4. Summarize the procedures that you used in this experiment so another person could repeat the experiment and get the same results.

    _____

    _____

    _____

    _____

    _____

    _____

    _____

Name: _____ Date: _____

Chapter 4: Organization of the Periodic Table: *The Scientific Method—Why Are Elements Put Into Families?*

5. What observations did you make about how different families react to ammonium compounds?

   _____

   _____

   _____

6. What can you conclude from this experiment?

   _____

   _____

   _____

7. What predictions can you make about how other elements in the alkali metal family will react to ammonium compounds?

   _____

   _____

   _____

8. What predictions can you make about how other elements in the alkaline earth metal family will react to ammonium compounds?

   _____

   _____

   _____

9. What was the variable (the thing that changed) in this experiment?

   _____

   _____

10. Name one thing that was controlled in this experiment.

   _____

   _____

Name: _____ Date: _____

Chapter 4: Organization of the Periodic Table: *Families of Elements Poster Activity*

_____

Family Name

Purpose: To produce a poster of an element family that shows the family's characteristics, uses, examples, and drawings of the characteristics and uses.

Materials: Colored markers, ruler, poster paper, periodic table, *The Families of Elements Resource Sheet*, the booklet titled *Uses of the Elements*, and any other resources that have element family information.

Procedures:

1. Research the family of elements that your teacher has assigned to your group.
2. Make a rough draft for a poster showing characteristics, uses, examples, and drawings of the family of elements that you have been assigned.
3. After your rough draft has been approved by your teacher, draw your final draft on a piece of poster paper using markers and a ruler.

Poster Rough Draft

Characteristics   Examples

_____   _____

_____   _____

_____   _____

_____   _____

_____   _____

Uses   Drawings

_____

_____

_____

_____

_____

Chapter 4: Organization of the Periodic Table: *Families of Elements Poster Activity Rubric*

Appearance (5 points)

5   The poster looks excellent. A ruler clearly was used. Printing was neat and in color. Drawings were clear and neat.

4   The poster looks good. A ruler clearly was used. Printing was neat and in color. Drawings were neat.

3   The poster looks average. A ruler may not have been used. Printing was readable. Color was used. Drawings were present.

2   The poster looks poor. A ruler was not used. Printing was difficult to read. Drawings and color were not used.

0-1   The poster looks bad. A ruler was not used. Printing could not be read. Drawings and color were not used. Poster was sloppily done in order to finish quickly.

Total Appearance Points (out of 5)   _____

Teaching Quality (5 points)

5   The poster teaches an excellent lesson about the family. The poster shows many characteristics, uses, examples, and drawings that relate to the family. A person knowing nothing about the family would benefit from looking at the poster.

4   The poster teaches a good lesson about the family. The poster shows good characteristics, uses, examples, and drawings that relate to the family. A person knowing nothing about the family would benefit from looking at the poster.

3   The poster teaches a lesson about the family. Some important uses, characteristics, examples, or drawings were left out or did not relate to the family.

0-2   The poster did not teach a lesson about the family. Sections were poorly done or missing.

Total Teaching Quality Points (out of 5)   _____

Planning (5 points)

5   An excellent plan was used to make the poster. The entire sheet of paper was used to make the poster.

4   A good plan was used to make the poster. Most of the paper was used.

3   An average plan was used. Parts of the paper went unused.

0-2   The plan was difficult to see or nonexistent.

Total Planning Points (out of 5)   _____

Chapter 4: Organization of the Periodic Table: *Families of Elements Poster Activity Rubric (cont.)*

Completeness (5 points)

5   All components of the poster were completed in the given amount of time.

4   One of the components was incomplete when posters were due.

0-3   More than one of the components of the poster was incomplete or missing when the poster was due.

Total Completeness Points (out of 5)   _____

Social Skills (5 points)

5   Excellent! Everybody participated. The group attended well to the teacher. Students used quiet voices and only worked with the members of their group. Students stayed on task.

4   Good! Students did a good job of following the above social skills.

3   Unsatisfactory! Students worked efficiently but from time to time violated one or more of the social skills.

0-2   Poor! Work was seriously impeded by frequent violations of the above social skills.

Total Social Skills Points (out of 5)   _____

Total Points Out of 25   _____

Percent Out of 100   _____

Final Group Grade on the Families Poster   A   B   C   D   F

Chapter 4: Organization of the Periodic Table: *The Families of Elements Resource Information*

Group 1: The Alkali Metal Family

The alkali metal family is found on the periodic table in Group 1, which is on the far left side of the table. The metals in this group are lithium, sodium, potassium, rubidium, cesium, and francium. The gas hydrogen is also put in this group because of its reactivity.

All of the metals in this group are soft, silvery-white metals with low melting points. These metals, along with hydrogen, are extremely reactive. Hydrogen will blow up upon any contact with flames. The metals are so reactive that they will burn the skin if touched. They tarnish rapidly. The metals in this family react violently with water. They easily form salts with the halogens. They are never found in their pure forms in nature. The metals in this family are easy to identify because they each give off a different color when they burn. Lithium flames are a crimson color, sodium flames are yellow, potassium flames are violet, rubidium flames are reddish-violet, and cesium flames are blue. Little is known about francium because it is so rare and radioactive.

The alkali metal family has many important uses. Lithium is used in grease and other lubricants. It is also used in aircraft parts and batteries. Sodium is found in salt, and used in gasoline. Potassium is more expensive than sodium and is less widely used. Potassium is used in fertilizer and photography. For more uses of the alkali metals, see the *Uses of the Elements* booklet.

Group 2: The Alkaline Earth Metal Family

The alkaline earth metal family is found on the periodic table in Group 2, which is on the far left side of the table between Group 1, the alkali metals, and Groups 3-12, the transition elements. This family is made up of six metals (beryllium, magnesium, calcium, strontium, barium, and radium).

The metals in this family are all soft and silvery-white in color. They have high melting points and high densities. They are reactive. They will react with water. They can be handled by humans. These metals will oxidize or tarnish in air. They are never found in nature in their pure forms. They are good conductors of electricity. Each element of this family burns in a different color. Magnesium will give off a bright white light. Calcium flames are an orange-red. Strontium flames give off a bright red color. Barium will burn with a yellowish-green color. Radium gives off a vivid crimson color when it burns.

The alkaline earth metals are used in fireworks because of their bright colors when they burn. Beryllium is often added to other metals to make hard metal alloys. Beryllium is also used to make rocket nose cones. Beryllium is used in nuclear reactors. Magnesium is used in aircraft and photographic equipment. Calcium is used with other metals to make reactive alloys. Radium is radioactive and is used in the treatment of cancer. For other uses of the alkaline earth metals, see the *Uses of the Elements* booklet.

Chapter 4: Organization of the Periodic Table: *The Families of Elements Resource Information*

Groups 3-12: The Transition Element Family

The transition element family is found in the middle of the periodic table in Groups 3-12. The transition element family is by far the largest family on the periodic table with 40 members. Some of the more common and widely-used members of this family include iron, nickel, copper, zinc, silver, and gold.

The transition elements are all metals; that's why they are sometimes called the transition metals. Most of the elements in this family are hard, strong, and shiny metals. Most of them have very high melting points and boiling points. Mercury is one exception; it is a liquid at room temperature. Most transition elements are good conductors of heat and electricity. Most transition elements will dissolve in acid. Gold is one exception; it resists acids. Most transition elements can bond to oxygen in more ways than one, making different compounds. Iron is a good example of this behavior. Iron bonds with oxygen to form the ores hematite and magnetite. Both ores have different ratios of oxygen and iron. Most of these elements can be pounded into shapes and drawn into wires. Most of the transition elements can form colored compounds with oxygen. Zinc, titanium, and chromium form many colored compounds with oxygen.

The transition elements have many uses because of their ability to form strong metal alloys, their ability to be pounded into shapes, their ability to be drawn into wires, and their beauty. It is because of these abilities that transition elements are used in construction materials, pipes, wires, coins, jewelry, aircraft, cars, bicycles, cooking utensils, and many other items. Many transition elements are used to manufacture widely-used compounds, such as cleaners. Many transitions elements are used in catalytic converters, which help control the pollution in car exhaust. Transition elements are also added to paints to give them color. For other uses of transition elements, see the *Uses of the Elements* booklet.

Chapter 4: Organization of the Periodic Table: *The Families of Elements Resource Information*

Groups 13-16: The BCNO Family

The BCNO family is found on the right side of the periodic table between the transition elements (Group 3-12) and the halogens (Group 17). The BCNO family is a very large family with 25 members. Some of the more common members of this family include carbon, nitrogen, oxygen, aluminum, silicon, sulfur, arsenic, tin, and lead.

The BCNO family is sometimes divided into two or even four separate families. This is by far the most diverse family of elements. The BCNO family is given its name because of the symbols of the lightest elements in each column of the family: boron (B), carbon (C), nitrogen (N), and oxygen (O). The members of this family are metals, nonmetals, or metalloids. Some members of this family are gases at room temperature (nitrogen and oxygen), but most are solids. They are reactive but are selective with which elements they will bond. Most will bond with oxygen. Oxygen will even bond with itself. There are no hard and fast rules that fit all the elements of this family except that the members of each column tend to bond with other elements in a similar fashion.

There is a wide variety of uses for the BCNO family. This is because there is a wide variety of elements. Many of the elements of the BCNO family are essential to life (carbon, oxygen, nitrogen, and phosphorus). The metals in this family are used in the electronics industry. Silicon and germanium are used in computers. The nonmetals in this family are used as insulators on wires because they will not conduct electricity. Some members in this family are used as poisons, fertilizers, in scuba gear, soap, glass-making, solder, aircraft, and weapons. Aluminum is a member of this family with many uses, including drink cans, foil, pots, and pans. For more uses of the BCNO family, see the *Uses of the Elements* booklet.

Chapter 4: Organization of the Periodic Table: *The Families of Elements Resource Information*

Group 17: The Halogen Family

The elements of Group 17, the halogens, are found on the right side of the periodic table between Groups 13-16 (the BCNO family) and Group 18 (the noble gases). The halogens are a very small family consisting of only five elements (fluorine, chlorine, bromine, iodine, and astatine).

The halogens are a family of poisonous nonmetals. At room temperature fluorine and chlorine are gases, bromine is a liquid, and iodine and astatine are solids. The halogens are very reactive and are never found in their pure forms in nature. The reactivity of the halogens decreases as atomic number increases. The halogens are poor conductors of electricity. The halogens will combine with the alkali metals to form a family of chemical compounds called salts.

The halogen family has a variety of uses. Fluorine is added to toothpaste and water to prevent tooth decay. Fluorine will combine with uranium to form nuclear fuel. Chlorine is added to water supplies and swimming pools to kill germs. Chlorine is widely used in bleach and salt. Bromine is used as a gasoline additive, photograph developer, fire retardant, and an insecticide. Bromine is also used to kill germs in water supplies. Iodine is added to salt to reduce thyroid disease. Iodine is also used as a film developer and as a disinfectant in water supplies. Astatine is very rare, very radioactive, and has no uses. For more uses of the halogen family, see the *Uses of the Elements* booklet.

Group 18: The Noble Gases

The noble gases are found in the far right column of the periodic table just to the right of Group 17, the halogens. The noble gases are a family of six gases: helium, neon, argon, krypton, xenon, and radon.

All of the members of the noble gas family are colorless, tasteless, and odorless gases. They are extremely nonreactive. Helium, neon, and argon will not combine with other elements. Xenon, krypton, and radon will combine with other elements, but this is a very difficult process to perform. When an electrical current is passed through one of these gases, it will glow in a characteristic color. Neon has a characteristic orange-red glow.

Helium is lighter than air and is used in balloons and blimps. Neon, argon, krypton, and xenon are used in lights because of the colors they make and in light bulbs because they do not react with the metal (usually tungsten) that makes up the filament. Radon is radioactive and is used in the treatment of cancer. For more uses of the noble gas family, see the *Uses of the Elements* booklet.

Chapter 4: Organization of the Periodic Table: *The Families of Elements Resource Information*

The Lanthanide Series

The lanthanide series of elements is found at the bottom of the periodic table. This series appears in the top of the bottom two rows. It consists of 15 elements, including lanthanum.

Every member of the lanthanide series is a soft, silvery metal. These metals are reactive and will burn in oxygen or air. They will oxidize or tarnish rapidly in air. The lanthanide series metals are similar to the metals in the transition elements family, except they are poor conductors of electricity. The lanthanides all react in a similar manner, and it is because of this that they are found together in nature. Lanthanides produce a spark when struck.

Lanthanide alloys made with iron are used to make flints for cigarette lighters because of their ability to produce a spark. Several of the metals in this series are used in glass, welders' goggles, nuclear reactors, and the petroleum industry. Many of the lanthanides are used in color television screens and computer monitors because they produce colors when combined with phosphorus. Some examples of the colors produced by lanthanides include red from europium and green from terbium. For more uses of the lanthanide series, see the *Uses of the Elements* booklet.

The Actinide Series

The actinide series of elements is found in the very bottom row of the periodic table. This series is made of 15 elements, including actinium and uranium.

The members of the actinide series are all radioactive. All of the actinides are silvery metals. All of the elements in the actinide series are reactive. Actinium, thorium, protactinium, and uranium are all natural. Neptunium and plutonium were once thought to be only synthetic, but small amounts have been found in nature. All other members of this series are synthetic. All of the actinides after curium are very radioactive and have been produced in such small amounts that little is known about these elements.

Uranium is by far the most stable actinide. It is used as a fuel for nuclear power plants and nuclear weapons. Uranium is also used as a pigment in glass and ceramics. Plutonium is used in nuclear weapons and to power space exploration equipment. Curium is used to power satellites and was used to test moon soils. Americium is used in smoke detectors. For more uses of the actinides, see the *Uses of the Elements* booklet.

96

Name: _____ Date: _____

Chapter 4: Organization of the Periodic Table: *The Families of Elements—Group Quiz*

Directions: Use the family posters created by your class, along with a periodic table, to answer the questions below with your group.

Part I. Examples: In the space provided, write the name of the family to which each element belongs.

1. Silver   _____   9. Plutonium   _____
2. Helium   _____   10. Lead   _____
3. Cerium   _____   11. Gold   _____
4. Sodium   _____   12. Sulfur   _____
5. Chlorine   _____   13. Argon   _____
6. Uranium   _____   14. Iodine   _____
7. Nitrogen   _____   15. Potassium   _____
8. Calcium   _____   16. Magnesium   _____

Part II. Element Uses: Give one use for each of the following elements.

17. Aluminum   _____
18. Sodium   _____
19. Fluorine   _____
20. Iodine   _____
21. Helium   _____
22. Terbium   _____
23. Uranium   _____
24. Beryllium _____
25. Calcium   _____
26. Argon   _____

Part III. Family Uses: Sometimes entire families of elements can be used for the same purpose. Give one use for each of the following families.

27. Alkaline Earth Metals   _____
28. Transition Elements   _____
29. Lanthanide Series   _____
30. Noble Gases   _____

Name: _____   Date: _____

Chapter 4: Organization of the Periodic Table: *The Families of Elements—Group Quiz (cont.)*

Part IV. Characteristics: Give one characteristic of each of the following families.

31. Alkali Metals   _____
32. Alkaline Earth Metals _____
33. Transition Elements   _____
34. BCNO Groups   _____
35. Halogens   _____
36. Noble Gases   _____
37. Lanthanide Series   _____
38. Actinide Series   _____

Part V. Drawings: Make a drawing that shows a characteristic, example, or use for each of the following families.

Alkali Metals	**Alkaline Earth Metals**	**Transition Elements**	**BCNO Group**

Halogens	**Noble Gases**	**Lanthanides**	**Actinides**

Review Activities: *The Teacher's Guide*

<u>Pages 100-114 - The Element Game</u>

This game is best played in cooperative groups of three to four students; however, up to nine students can play on one board at once.

The board for the game appears as four separate pieces on pages 100 to 103. You may want to enlarge each section of the board by the same percentage on an 11" x 17" sheet of paper before connecting the pieces to form the complete board. Once you have copied and/or enlarged each section, lay the sections out on a table or desktop to see where the sections should join. You may need to use a straight edge to mark where to cut the excess off some sections so that the picture joins smoothly. Then tape the pieces together. If the outside edge of the board is jagged, use the straight edge to mark the excess that needs to be cut off. Make enough boards for each group. The boards are best used when they are laminated to a piece of cardboard or construction paper.

Page 104 outlines the rules for the game. Teachers should make one copy of the rules for each group; it works best to laminate this page also. Page 105 has the tokens for the game. Teachers may want to reduce this page in the copier when they make one copy for each group. The tokens should be laminated and cut out prior to playing the game. There are 20 Mendeleyev coins on page 106. It is best to have at least one page of coins per student. Have these copied on a sheet of colored paper and have the kids cut them out. Pages 107-114 are the question cards for the game. The cards come in four categories, which include element history, element properties, uses of elements, and element families. There are 16 question cards in each category. Each sheet of cards should be reproduced and made available for each group. The teacher should write the category on the back of each card. When duplicating the cards, teachers may want to use different colors of card stock for each category. The cards should be laminated and cut out.

This game requires a lot of preparation. It is best to have the students help in the preparation of the game. Once the games have been made, they can be easily stored for the future. The game is a good review activity for the periodic table and the elements. It is also fun for the students. An extension for this game can include students making their own questions for the game.

<u>Pages 115-118 - Elements and the Periodic Table Test</u>

This test is designed as a written form of evaluation for the unit on elements and the periodic table. Teachers may decide to let students use some or all of the resources in this book. Teachers may want to make other resources available to the students. Teachers may also decide not to let students use any resources. The test is best administered individually to the students and graded by the teacher.

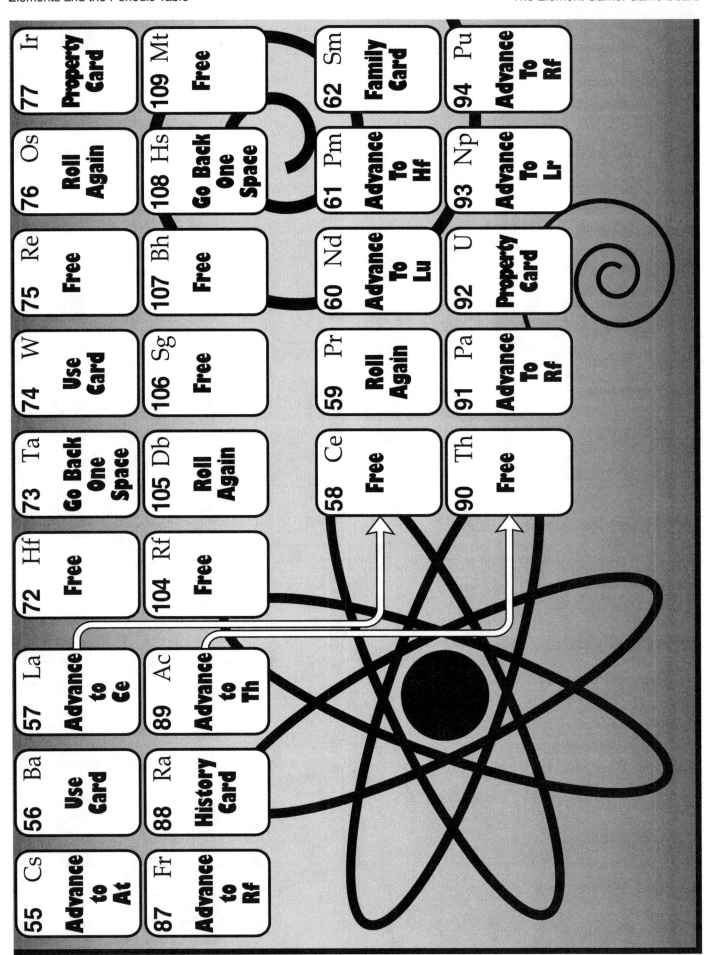

The Element Game: *Rules*

How to Play the Game:

1. Each player in the group selects one token and receives ten Mendeleyev coins.

2. Each player places his or her token on the start (hydrogen) space on the element game board.

3. Everybody rolls the dice to see who goes first. The highest number goes first. Turns proceed to the right of the person who starts.

4. Roll the dice. Move that many spaces and do what it says on each element on the board.

5. **Free spaces:** If you land on a free space, your turn is over. You don't have to do anything.

6. **Card spaces:** If you land on a card space, have another person in the group draw a card from that category (property, history, family, or use). That person will read the question to you. You must answer the question in ten seconds. If you answer the question correctly, you will receive one Mendeleyev coin. If you answer incorrectly, you must pay one Mendeleyev coin. If you fail to answer the question in the ten seconds, you must pay two Mendeleyev coins.

7. **Roll again spaces:** You may roll the dice again.

8. **Go back spaces:** You must go back the number of spaces indicated on the board.

9. **Advance spaces:** You may advance your token to the element indicated on the board.

10. **Ending the Game:**
    A.   The first person to complete the board by reaching element 112 exactly becomes the reader and will read all further questions. The first person to finish will also receive three Mendeleyev coins.
    B.   If you do not land on element 112 exactly, you must go back to your last space and remain in the game until you land on element 112.
    C.   As each person finishes, he or she may help with reading the questions.
    D.   The second player to finish will receive two Mendeleyev coins. Each person who finishes after the second finisher will receive one Mendeleyev coin when they land on element 112.

11. **Winning the game:** When all players have finished the board, the person with the most Mendeleyev coins wins.

The Element Game: *Game Tokens*

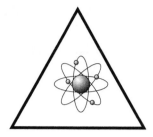

Element Game Token

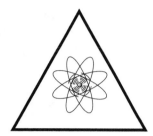

Element Game Token

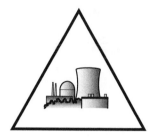

Element Game Token

Element Game Token

Element Game Token

Element Game Token

Element Game Token

Element Game Token

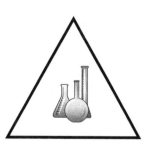

Element Game Token

The Element Game: *Mendeleyev Coins*

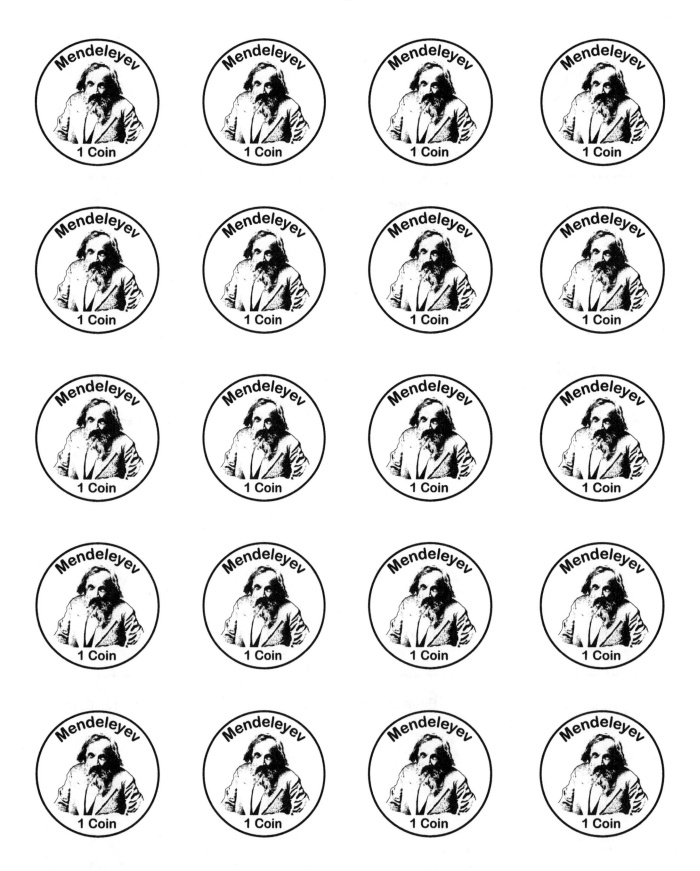

The Element Game: *Game Cards*

Element History
What year did Glen Seaborg discover plutonium?
A. 1898
B. 1921
C. 1941
D. 1961
(Answer: C. 1941)

Element History
Which scientist discovered nuclear fission with her nephew Otto Frisch?
A. Marie Curie
B. Shirley Jackson
C. Irene Joliot-Curie
D. Lise Meitner
(Answer: D. Lise Meitner)

Element History
Marie and Pierre Curie discovered two new elements in 1889. They were radium and _____.
A. Actinium
B. Neon
C. Plutonium
D. Polonium
(Answer: D. Polonium)

Element History
Which of the following elements was discovered on the sun before it was discovered on earth?
A. Helium
B. Hydrogen
C. Technetium
D. Uranium
(Answer: A. Helium)

Element History
All of these elements were known by ancient civilizations except _____.
A. Carbon
B. Gold
C. Iodine
D. Sulfur
(Answer: C. Iodine)

Element History
What war ended with the use of atomic bombs?
A. World War I
B. World War II
C. The Korean Conflict
D. The Vietnam Crisis
(Answer: B. World War II)

Element History
When did the most serious nuclear accident in the U.S. happen at Three Mile Island in Pennsylvania?
A. 1945
B. 1954
C. 1979
D. 1997
(Answer: C. 1979)

Element History
What year was the first nuclear power station opened?
A. 1947
B. 1957
C. 1965
D. 1977
(Answer: B. 1957)

Element History

Which element was used by the ancient Egyptians, in the form of borax, to make mummies?
A. Arsenic
B. Carbon
C. Chlorine
D. Sodium
(Answer: D. Sodium)

Element History

What year did the California Gold Rush begin?
A. 1848
B. 1865
C. 1900
D. 1936
(Answer: A. 1848)

Element History

What element did the ancient Romans alloy with copper to make armor?
A. Chromium
B. Iron
C. Nickel
D. Zinc
(Answer: D. Zinc)

Element History

What element did ancient alchemists think they could make into gold?
A. Carbon
B. Lead
C. Silver
D. Zinc
(Answer: B. Lead)

Element History

What element was found in 1669 because it glowed in distilled urine?
A. Fluorine
B. Phosphorus
C. Radium
D. Uranium
(Answer: B. Phosphorus)

Element History

What year did the hydrogen balloon *Hindenburg* explode and kill 35 people?
A. 1783
B. 1937
C. 1956
D. 1981
(Answer: B. 1937)

Element History

What element was used by ancient Chinese civilizations as an explosive?
A. Carbon
B. Hydrogen
C. Magnesium
D. Sulfur
(Answer: D. Sulfur)

Element History

What element known by the ancients began to be used, in about 1946, to date rocks and fossils?
A. Boron
B. Carbon
C. Lead
D. Silicon
(Answer: B. Carbon)

108

Element Properties

At room temperature most elements are _____.
A. Gases
B. Liquids
C. Solids
(Answer: C. Solids)

Element Properties

The two elements that are liquid at room temperature are bromine and _____.
A. Alcohol
B. Iodine
C. Mercury
D. Water
(Answer: C. Mercury)

Element Properties

Which of the following elements is a metalloid?
A. Fluorine
B. Iron
C. Silicon
D. Sodium
(Answer: C. Silicon)

Element Properties

This is a friendly element. It will bond with almost every other element.
A. Chlorine
B. Iron
C. Oxygen
D. Silver
(Answer: C. Oxygen)

Element Properties

All of the isotopes of this element are radioactive.
A. Barium
B. Cesium
C. Radium
D. Strontium
(Answer: C. Radium)

Element Properties

Metals can be pounded into shapes and are good conductors of heat and _____.
A. Electricity
B. Isotopes
C. Magnetism
D. Radiation
(Answer: A. Electricity)

Element Properties

When iron reacts with oxygen, it forms _____.
A. A magnet
B. An isotope
C. Cobalt metal
D. Rust
(Answer: D. Rust)

Element Properties

The atomic number of an element is the same as the _____.
A. Atomic mass
B. Atomic mass number
C. Element family
D. Number of protons
(Answer: D. Number of protons)

Element Properties
Which of the following elements can be found in nature in its pure form?
A. Chromium
B. Gold
C. Sodium
D. Zinc
(Answer: B. Gold)

Element Properties
Which of the following gases has a yellow color and an irritating odor?
A. Chlorine
B. Helium
C. Hydrogen
D. Oxygen
(Answer: A. Chlorine)

Element Properties
Which of the following gases is highly flammable?
A. Helium
B. Hydrogen
C. Krypton
D. Neon
(Answer: B. Hydrogen)

Element Properties
Which element is the most abundant element in the earth's crust?
A. Aluminum
B. Carbon
C. Oxygen
D. Silicon
(Answer: C. Oxygen)

Element Properties
Which element is the most common element in the human body?
A. Carbon
B. Hydrogen
C. Oxygen
D. Nitrogen
(Answer: B. Hydrogen)

Element Properties
Which element is the most common element in the universe?
A. Helium
B. Hydrogen
C. Oxygen
D. Titanium
(Answer: B. Hydrogen)

Element Properties
What results when two or more elements combine chemically?
A. Allotropes
B. Alloys
C. Compounds
D. Isotopes
(Answer: C. Compounds)

Element Properties
Diamonds are the hardest substances known. What element makes diamonds?
A. Carbon
B. Chromium
C. Iron
D. Uranium
(Answer: A. Carbon)

Uses of Elements

Which element is used to make drink cans?
A. Aluminum
B. Lead
C. Iron
D. Tin
(Answer: A. Aluminum)

Uses of Elements

I'm the element used in blimps today.
I am _____.
A. Chlorine
B. Helium
C. Hydrogen
D. Neon
(Answer: B. Helium)

Uses of Elements

Which element gives emeralds their color?
A. Carbon
B. Beryllium
C. Silicon
D. Zirconium
(Answer: B. Beryllium)

Uses of Elements

Which of the following gases makes up 78% of air?
A. Carbon Dioxide
B. Nitrogen
C. Oxygen
D. Water Vapor
(Answer: B. Nitrogen)

Uses of Elements

Which element am I? I'm used to make fireworks.
A. Chromium
B. Krypton
C. Magnesium
D. Neon
(Answer: C. Magnesium)

Uses of Elements

Which of the following elements is used as a superconductor?
A. Aluminum
B. Carbon
C. Hydrogen
D. Yttrium
(Answer: D. Yttrium)

Uses of Elements

Who am I? I'm used to make non-stick coating for pots and pans.
A. Aluminum
B. Fluorine
C. Mercury
D. Silicon
(Answer: B. Fluorine)

Uses of Elements

Which of the following elements is used in swimming pools to kill germs?
A. Arsenic
B. Boron
C. Chlorine
D. Uranium
(Answer: C. Chlorine)

Uses of Elements

This element is used as the main fuel in nuclear power plants.
A. Mercury
B. Neptunium
C. Plutonium
D. Uranium
(Answer: D. Uranium)

Uses of Elements

Who am I? I am used to find diseases in the thyroid gland.
A. Barium
B. Iodine
C. Radium
D. Rhodium
(Answer: B. Iodine)

Uses of Elements

Who am I? I'm used in water pipes, wires, coins, and I coat a U.S. penny.
A. Copper
B. Gold
C. Silver
D. Zinc
(Answer: A. Copper)

Uses of Elements

Who am I? I make up about 25% of the U.S. five-cent piece.
A. Copper
B. Nickel
C. Silver
D. Steel
(Answer: B. Nickel)

Uses of Elements

Which of the following elements is used to make the filament in light bulbs?
A. Antimony
B. Argon
C. Chromium
D. Tungsten
(Answer: D. Tungsten)

Uses of Elements

Who are we? We are the two elements that make up water.
A. Carbon and Mercury
B. Hydrogen and Oxygen
C. Hydrogen and Water
D. Oxygen and Silicon
(Answer: B. Hydrogen and Oxygen)

Uses of Elements

Who am I? I'm very good at detecting smoke in your house.
A. Americium
B. Nitrogen
C. Sulfur
D. Thorium
(Answer: A. Americium)

Uses of Elements

Who are we? We are the two elements used to make regular table salt.
A. Chlorine and Sodium
B. Hydrogen and Oxygen
C. Iodine and Potassium
D. Lead and Lithium
(Answer: A. Chlorine and Sodium)

Element Families

Which of the following families contains boron, carbon, nitrogen, and oxygen?

A. Alkali Metals
B. BCNO Group
C. Lanthanides
D. Noble Gases

(Answer: B. BCNO Group)

Element Families

Which of the following families will burn your skin if you touch them?

A. Actinides
B. Alkali Metals
C. Alkaline Earths
D. Transition Elements

(Answer: B. Alkali Metals)

Element Families

This family is found on the very bottom of the periodic table.

A. Actinides
B. Halogens
C. Lanthanides
D. Transition Elements

(Answer: A. Actinides)

Element Families

Name the family that is found on the far left-hand side of the periodic table.

A. Alkali Metals
B. BCNO Group
C. Halogens
D. Noble Gases

(Answer: A. Alkali Metals)

Element Families

Which of the following families contains all metals?

A. BCNO Group
B. Halogens
C. Noble Gases
D. Transition Elements

(Answer: D. Transition Elements)

Element Families

The elements of this family are found together in nature.

A. Actinides
B. BCNO Group
C. Halogens
D. Lanthanides

(Answer: D. Lanthanides)

Element Families

Which of the following families is made up of poisonous nonmetals?

A. Alkali Metals
B. Alkaline Earth Metals
C. Halogens
D. Lanthanides

(Answer: C. Halogens)

Element Families

Which of the following families is the least reactive of all element families?

A. Alkali Earth Metals
B. Halogens
C. Noble Gases
D. Transition Elements

(Answer: C. Noble Gases)

113

Element Families

Which of the following families has every member radioactive?
A. Actinides
B. Lanthanides
C. Noble Gases
D. Transition Elements
(Answer: A. Actinides)

Element Families

Which element family is found on the far right-hand side of the periodic table?
A. Alkali Metals
B. Halogens
C. Lanthanides
D. Noble Gases
(Answer: D. Noble Gases)

Element Families

This family is used in fireworks because they burn in bright colors.
A. Alkaline Earth Metals
B. Halogens
C. Lanthanides
D. Transition Elements
(Answer: A. Alkaline Earth Metals)

Element Families

Calcium and magnesium belong to this family.
A. Actinides
B. Alkali Metals
C. Alkaline Earth Metals
D. BCNO Group
(Answer: C. Alkaline Earth Metals)

Element Families

Which is the largest (most members) element family?
A. Actinides
B. Lanthanides
C. Halogens
D. Transition Elements
(Answer: D. Transition Elements)

Element Families

This family combines with the alkali metals to form salts.
A. Actinides
B. Alkaline Earth Metals
C. Halogens
D. Noble Gases
(Answer: C. Halogens)

Element Families

This group is sometimes divided into two or even four families.
A. BCNO Group
B. Halogens
C. Lanthanides
D. Transition Elements
(Answer: A. BCNO Group)

Element Families

This metal family will make a spark when it is struck.
A. Alkali Metals
B. Alkaline Earth Metals
C. Lanthanides
D. Transition Elements
(Answer: C. Lanthanides)

Name: _____ Date: _____

Elements and the Periodic Table: *Test*

Directions: Use the periodic table to answer the following questions about elements and the periodic table.

Part I. Matching: Match the choices to the statements. Use each choice once.

_____	1.	The number of protons in an atom
_____	2.	Elements that are made in the lab
_____	3.	Elements that give off particles
_____	4.	He drew the first periodic table.
_____	5.	A positively charged particle in an atom
_____	6.	Tiny structures found in all matter
_____	7.	The vertical columns in the periodic table
_____	8.	The horizontal rows in the periodic table
_____	9.	Only bromine and mercury are this state of matter at room temperature.
_____	10.	These substances are made of one kind of atom.
_____	11.	Two or more elements or compounds physically together
_____	12.	Hydrogen, helium, and chlorine are in this state of matter.
_____	13.	This shows all the elements organized by their properties.
_____	14.	Two or more atoms that are chemically bonded
_____	15.	Elements that have characteristics of both metals and nonmetals
_____	16.	Most of the elements are in this state of matter at room temperature.
_____	17.	Every element has one of these. It usually has two letters, but some have one or three letters.
_____	18.	These conduct heat and electricity. They have a shiny luster. They can be pounded into shapes or drawn into wires.
_____	19.	They tried to combine science and magic. They tried to change lead into gold. They discovered the scientific method.
_____	20.	These are poor conductors of heat and electricity. They have a dull luster. When pounded, they form powders or get shattered.

A. Alchemists
B. Atomic Number
C. Atoms
D. Compound
E. Elements
F. Element Family
G. Gas
H. Liquid
I. Mendeleyev
J. Metals
K. Metalloid
L. Mixture
M. Nonmetals
N. Period
O. Periodic Table
P. Proton
Q. Radioactive
R. Solid
S. Symbol
T. Synthetic

Name: _____ Date: _____

Elements and the Periodic Table: *Test (cont.)*

Part II. Know Your Symbols: Write the symbols for each of the following elements in the space provided.

_____ 21. Iron

_____ 22. Calcium

_____ 23. Iodine

_____ 24. Magnesium

_____ 25. Uranium

_____ 26. Potassium

_____ 27. Silver

_____ 28. Helium

_____ 29. Phosphorus

_____ 30. Carbon

Part III. Element Families: Below is a list of characteristics and examples of the element families. Write the name of the element family in the space provided. Use the family once or more than once.

_____ 31. These elements are all tasteless, colorless, and odorless gases.

_____ 32. These elements are all radioactive.

_____ 33. These elements are good conductors of heat and electricity, like gold and silver.

_____ 34. These soft metals will burn your skin.

_____ 35. These reactive metals will produce a spark when they are struck.

_____ 36. Metals like calcium and magnesium belong to this family

_____ 37. This family has members that are metals, nonmetals, and metalloids.

_____ 38. These combine with alkali metals to form salts.

_____ 39. Metals like iron, copper, and zinc belong to this large family.

_____ 40. This family is found in the far right column of the periodic table.

Part IV. Uses: Write one use for each of the following elements.

41. Aluminum _____

42. Hydrogen _____

43. Argon _____

44. Silicon _____

45. Americium _____

46. Lithium _____

47. Carbon _____

48. Fluorine _____

49. Gold _____

50. Tungsten _____

Name: _____ Date: _____

Elements and the Periodic Table: *Test (cont.)*

Part V. Time Line: Below is a list of synthetic elements and their discovery dates. Use a ruler to construct a time line showing each element and its discovery date. Do not write in the grading section. This is for teacher use only.

Synthetic Elements

Element	Discovery Date
Berkelium	1949
Curium	1944
Einsteinium	1952
Lawrencium	1961
Plutonium	1940

Grading Section

Scale (2)	_____
Title (2)	_____
Neatness (2)	_____
Completeness (2)	_____
Correct (2)	_____
Total (10)	_____

_____

Time Line Title

Name: _____ Date: _____

Elements and the Periodic Table: *Test (cont.)*

Part VI. Graphing: Below is a list of elements and compounds that are found in the air and their percentages. Use a ruler to construct a bar graph of those elements and compounds and their percentages. Do not write in the grading section. This is for teacher use only.

Elements in the Air

Element	Percentage
Nitrogen	78.00%
Oxygen	20.90%
Argon	0.90%
Others	0.17%
Carbon dioxide	0.03%

Grading Section

Title (2)	_____
Neatness (2)	_____
Scale and Label (2)	_____
Plan (2)	_____
Correct (2)	_____
Total (10)	_____

_____

Graph Title

Answer Keys

Chapter 1
Page 16 - Getting to Know You - The Periodic Table
Answers will vary on this page. Expect students to use familiar elements such as gold, silver, oxygen, and iron.

Page 18 - Element, Compound, or Mixture
Matching

1. E	6. M	11. M	16. M
2. M	7. C	12. M	17. M
3. E	8. M	13. M	18. E
4. C	9. M	14. C	19. M
5. C	10. M	15. M	20. E

Listing Sections - Answers will vary.

Page 19 - Where are the Elements? - The Body
Answers will vary. See Part V. Graphing at the end of this section for an example.

Page 22 - Time Line Practice
Teacher check. Construction of time lines may vary. Elements should be in the following order.

1669 - Phosphorus
1766 - Hydrogen
1789 - Uranium
1807 - Sodium
1824 - Silicon
1886 - Fluorine
1895 - Helium
1900 - Radon
1923 - Hafnium
1940 - Plutonium
1961 - Lawrencium
1970 - Dubnium
1982 - Meitnerium
1996 - Ununbium

Page 23 - Element Time Line Construction
Teacher check. Construction of time lines will vary. Elements and their uses should be listed in chronological order.

Page 25 - Naming the Elements

1. F	6. L	11. V	16. G
2. B	7. Y	12. W	17. I
3. D	8. R	13. C	18. S
4. U	9. T	14. O	19. N
5. M	10. H	15. E	20. A
			21. P

Page 26 - Hidden Messages
1. Many elements are given names from other languages.
2. Some elements were named by the ancient people who used them.

Pages 27-29 - What Are Elements? Quiz
Part I. Using Words
1. Answers will vary. Here's a possible answer. The <u>elements</u> found in the universe are <u>organized</u> on the <u>periodic table</u>.
2. Answers will vary. Here's a possible answer. <u>Elements</u> and <u>compounds</u> are both pure substances. All other substances are <u>mixtures</u> of <u>elements</u> and <u>compounds</u>.

Part II. Matching		Part III. Element or Non-element	
3. E	9. A	15. N	20. N
4. I	10. J	16. E	21. N
5. G	11. D	17. E	22. E
6. B	12. H	18. N	23. N
7. F	13. K	19. E	24. E
8. L	14. C		

Part IV. Time Line
Teacher check. Construction of time lines will vary. Events should be listed in chronological order.

Part V. Graphing.
Teacher check. Graphs will vary. Below is a possible bar graph.

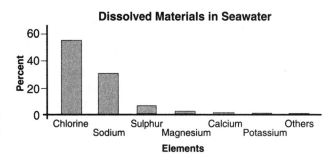

© Mark Twain Media, Inc., Publishers

Chapter 2
Page 43 - Periodic Pictures
Many possible answers. Here are a few examples.
1. Helium, hydrogen
2. Gallium, rhenium, mercury
3. Beryllium, carbon, aluminum, silicon, chromium, copper, zirconium, ytterbium, platinum, gold, silver
4. Fluorine
5. Silicon, zinc, gallium, germanium, gadolinium, terbium, tantalum, tungsten
6. Nickel, copper, silver, zinc, gold, lead
7. Hydrogen, boron, fluorine, sodium, vanadium, zirconium, niobium, cadmium, indium, lanthanum, gadolinium, dysprosium, hafnium, lead, uranium, plutonium
8. Lithium, magnesium, aluminum, scandium, titanium, niobium, praseodymium, gadolinium, tantalum, platinum
9. Silicon, phosphorus, zinc, rubidium, yttrium, europium, gadolinium, terbium, dysprosium, tungsten, lead
10. Helium, oxygen, potassium
11. Beryllium, cobalt, promethium, gadolinium, terbium, thulium, lead
12. Manganese
13. Fluorine, tantalum, iridium, platinum, gold
14. Carbon, chlorine, arsenic, strontium, cadmium, mercury, thallium, lead, radon

Page 44 - Places and Things.
Answers will vary. Here are a few examples.
A. Lithium, nitrogen, fluorine, sodium, magnesium, silicon, calcium, titanium, chromium, cobalt, arsenic, selenium, niobium, molybdenum, technetium, palladium, iodine, barium, promethium, terbium, tantalum, iridium, platinum, gold, thallium, bismuth, radon, radium
B. Lithium, selenium, bromine, krypton, silver, iodine, xenon, barium, cerium, tantalum, polonium
C. Hydrogen, boron, fluorine, sodium, vanadium, zirconium, niobium, cadmium, indium, lanthanum, gadolinium, dysprosium, hafnium, lead, uranium, plutonium, americium
D. Hydrogen, helium, lithium, beryllium, oxygen, aluminum, silicon, zirconium, niobium, iridium, gold, plutonium, curium
E. Lithium, sulfur, potassium, manganese, nickel, cadmium, mercury
F. Lithium, magnesium, aluminum, scandium, titanium, niobium, praseodymium, gadolinium, tantalum, platinum
G. Beryllium, carbon, aluminum, silicon, chromium, copper, zirconium, ytterbium, platinum, gold

H. Boron, fluorine, silicon, cobalt, gold, neodymium, samarium, holmium, erbium, lead
I. Nickel, copper, zinc, gold, lead
J. Boron, hydrogen, lithium, carbon, nitrogen, oxygen, fluorine, neon, sodium, magnesium, aluminum, silicon, phosphorus, sulfur, chlorine, argon, potassium, calcium, titanium, vanadium, chromium, manganese, iron, cobalt, nickel, copper, zinc, germanium, arsenic, selenium, rhodium, silver, tin, antimony, iodine, cerium, rhenium, osmium, mercury, americium

Pages 45-57 - Create a Table - Element Uses Group Work
Answers will vary. Look for neat, colorful, and well-researched work.

Page 58 Element Uses Crossword

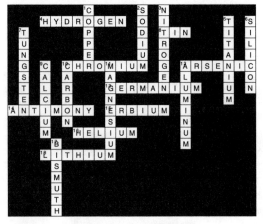

Page 59 - Element Uses Review
1. H   6. J   11. M
2. F   7. L   12. A
3. D   8. C   13. E
4. N   9. O   14. I
5. K   10. G   15. B

For 16-25, answers will vary.
16. **Aluminum**
Used for aluminum foil
Used in airplane wings
Used in sandpaper and grinding tools
Used to make fire bricks for ovens and furnaces
Is used to protect spark plugs and transistors
Is used in cosmetics for creams and lotions
Aluminum makes several jewelry items such as rubies and sapphires.
Aluminum can conduct electricity. It is used in wires, reflectors, resistors, antennas, and solar mirrors.
When combined with copper, it is used in construction material.
Is used to make drink cans, pots, and pans
Aluminum can be recycled.
Aluminum is used in some doors, screens, and window frames.

17. **Lanthanum**
Lanthanum is used in searchlights, movie projectors, and studio lighting.
Lanthanum isotopes are used in nuclear reactions.

18. **Iron**
Iron is used in many products containing steel. Such uses include cars, tools, appliances, chains, and cooking utensils.
Iron is used in buildings, bridges, and towers.
Iron is used in magnets.

19. **Oxygen**
We use oxygen to breathe.
Every cell in the body needs oxygen.
Oxygen makes ozone, which protects us from the harmful rays of the sun.
Combines with hydrogen to make water
Combines with just about every element to make a family of compounds called oxides
Makes hydrogen peroxide, which is used as an industrial and cosmetic bleach and disinfectant
Is used as a liquid rocket fuel

20. **Carbon**
Many organic compounds are made from carbon.
Many products such as petroleum and perfume are made from carbon.
Natural diamonds are made of carbon.
Graphite is made of carbon. Graphite is used in many products, such as pencils and synthetic diamonds.
Makes coal which is used to make heat and electricity in some areas
Carbon is combined with oxygen to form carbon dioxide. Carbon dioxide is exhaled when we breathe, used in photosynthesis, used for carbonation in soft drinks, and used to make decaffeinated coffee.
Dry ice is frozen carbon dioxide. Dry ice is used to freeze many things, such as ice cream.
Carbon is used to remove pollutants from the air.
Used in some inks, tires, and dry cells
Carbon combines with nitrogen to make cyanide, which is a very toxic poison.
Isotopes are used to date rocks and fossils.

21. **Gold**
Gold is used for money in the form of coins and bars.
Gold is used by dentists to fill teeth.
Gold is used to coat large glass plates and spacecraft.
Gold is used to make jewelry such as rings and necklaces.
Isotopes of gold are used to treat certain types of cancer.

22. **Lead**
In ancient times lead was used in coins, sculpture, and pipes.
Lead metal is used today in batteries, solder, and television screens.

Compounds of lead were used in paint and gasoline, but because of the high toxicity of lead, they are no longer used for these purposes.
Oxides of lead are used to make decorative glass called crystal.
Alloys of lead are used for printing type and as a radiation shield in nuclear power plants and X-ray machines.
Isotopes of lead are used to determine the age of rocks.

23. **Copper**
Copper makes excellent water pipes and electrical wires.
Copper is used in many of the U. S. coins, including coating the penny.
Copper is used in buttons on police uniforms (that's where the term for police copper, or cop, came from).
The Statue of Liberty is made in part of copper.
Copper is used in jewelry.
Copper is combined with other metals to make alloys such as brass and bronze, which are used to make a variety of products, including weapons, art pieces, and musical instruments, such as trumpets and trombones.
Copper is used in paint for ships.

24. **Silicon**
Makes up gemstones such as opal, amethyst, agate, and jasper
Makes up flint, which ancients used for tools and weapons
Ancients also used flint to start their fires.
Silicon makes up quartz, which is used in clocks and watches.
Quartz crystals are also used for control devices for television and radio transmitters.
Silicon is used in the production of glass, eyeglass lenses, and lenses for telescopes and microscopes.
Pyrex™ is made from a combination of silicon and boron. Pyrex™ is used in baking dishes, measuring cups, beakers, and test tubes.
Silicon is used to make ceramics, pottery, and china.
Silicon is used in transistors and solar cells.
Silicon is used in cosmetic surgery.
Silicon chips are used in computers to store information.

25. **Chlorine**
Was used in World War I as a poison gas
Chlorine is used as a germ killer in swimming pools and water supplies.
Chlorine is used in bleach.
Chlorine is used to make plastic pipes.
Hydrochloric acid is a chlorine compound used for cleaning the rust off metal and is used in the stomach for digesting food.

Chlorine is used in insecticides.
It was used in air conditioners and refrigerators until recently when it was discovered that chlorine is a pollutant.

Pages 60-61 - Uses of Elements Quiz
Answers will vary. Here are a few possible answers.
Part I: *Harlan's Day*
Mercury - Is used in older thermometers
Potassium - Harlan used soap in the shower.
Fluorine - Is found in toothpaste
Selenium - Is used in dandruff shampoos
Hydrogen - Is used in margarine for Harlan's toast
Americium - Harlan set off the smoke detector.
Zinc, silver, and copper - Are used in coins
Copper - Buttons on police uniforms from the social studies lesson
Bismuth - Used in the fire alarm at school
Selenium - Used in the robotics arm in tech. ed.
Silicon - Used in computers
Antimony - Used to make credit cards used in tech. ed.
Aluminum - Used in soda cans
Copper -Used to make brass trumpets
Silver - Used in photo development
Silicon - Used in beakers, test tubes, and computer chips
Radium - Used in cancer treatment
Nitrogen - Used to detect brain disorders
Zinc - Used in remote-controlled toys

Part II: You Make the Comic Strip
Answers will vary. Comics should look neat and the pictures should clearly show how one element is used.

Chapter 3
Page 64 - Element Symbols You Should Know
1. Al | 8. H | 14. Ni | 20. Ag
2. Ca | 9. I | 15. N | 21. Na
3. C | 10. Fe | 16. O | 22. S
4. Cl | 11. Pb | 17. P | 23. Sn
5. Cu | 12. Mg | 18. K | 24. U
6. Au | 13. Hg | 19. Si | 25. Zn
7. He

Pages 65-66 - Symbols To Know
1. The 25 elements listed should be properly placed on Periodic Table A.
2. Periodic Table B should be colored to show a distinction between solids, liquids, and gases. Answers will vary in number 2.
3. The chart should look as follows:

Element	Symbol	Atomic Number
Chromium	Cr	24
Titanium	Ti	22
Beryllium	Be	4
Strontium	Sr	38

Arsenic	As	33
Neon	Ne	10
Argon	Ar	18
Fluorine	F	9
Cobalt	Co	27
Lithium	Li	3

Pages 67-68 - Element Symbols Practice
Symbols Present - Cu, K, Fe, He, Hg, N, Na, Al, H, C, Au, U, S, Ni, O, Ag, P, Pb
Elements Present - Hydrogen, Potassium, Lead, Chlorine, Phosphorus, Silicon, Magnesium, Calcium, Mercury, Aluminum, Silver, Nitrogen, Sulfur, Zinc, Tin, Iodine, Gold
Symbols Missing - Ca, Cl, I, Mg, Si, Sn, Zn
Elements Missing - Carbon, Copper, Helium, Iron, Nickel, Oxygen, Sodium, Uranium

Page 68
The cooperative groups should have the 25 element names correctly taped to the 25 symbols on the colored sheet of paper.

Page 70 - Element Symbols Create a Phrase
Answers will vary.

Page 71 - Names and Symbols Do Not Match
1. J | 5. H | 9. G
2. C | 6. E | 10. I
3. B | 7. F | 11. K
4. D | 8. A

12-22. Answers will vary. Here are a few suggestions.
12. Sd | 16. Sv | 20. G
13. Ps | 17. T | 21. M
14. Io | 18. A | 22. L
15. Cp | 19. Tu

Page 72 - Symbols Practice Quiz I
1. Mg | 8. Cu | 14. I | 20. Sn
2. Au | 9. Na | 15. P | 21. Ag
3. H | 10. Ni | 16. Cl | 22. Hg
4. C | 11. Al | 17. Ca | 23. K
5. O | 12. Zn | 18. Fe | 24. N
6. S | 13. U | 19. He | 25. Pb
7. Si

26. Silver | 35. Helium | 43. Oxygen
27. Aluminum | 36. Mercury | 44. Phosphorus
28. Gold | 37. Iodine | 45. Lead
29. Carbon | 38. Potassium | 46. Sulfur
30. Calcium | 39. Magnesium | 47. Silicon
31. Chlorine | 40. Nitrogen | 48. Tin
32. Copper | 41. Sodium | 49. Uranium
33. Iron | 42. Nickel | 50. Zinc
34. Hydrogen

Page 73 - Symbols Practice Quiz II

1. Ni	10. Au	18. H
2. Nitrogen	11. Al	19. Lead
3. Mercury	12. Calcium	20. Magnesium
4. Fe	13. Carbon	21. Oxygen
5. Ag	14. Chlorine	22. P
6. K	15. Copper	22. Zn
7. Sulfur	16. Na	24. I
8. Silicon	17. He	25. U
9. Tin		

Page 74 - Symbols Practice Quiz III

1. I	8. H	14. B	20. A
2. J	9. Q	15. V	21. C
3. D	10. G	16. S	22. K
4. O	11. Y	17. U	23. T
5. R	12. M	18. F	24. X
6. P	13. E	19. L	25. W
7. N			

Pages 75-76 - Element Symbols - Test
Part I: Sentences

1. Hg	8. N	14. Sn	20. Na
2. U	9. Mg	15. I	21. Fe
3. Ca	10. Si	16. Pb	22. P
4. C	11. K	17. Au	23. H
5. He	12. S	18. Ag	24. Al
6. O	13. Cu	19. Zn	25. Ni
7. Cl			

Part II: Formulas

26. Oxygen	31. Carbon
27. Sodium	32. Silver
28. Hydrogen	33. Nitrogen
29. Silicon	34. Sulfur
30. Iron	35. Chlorine

Part III: Symbols

36. Iodine	44. Phosphorus
37. Magnesium	45. Potassium
38. Mercury	46. Copper
39. Gold	47. Zinc
40. Aluminum	48. Calcium
41. Nickel	49. Helium
42. Tin	50. Uranium
43. Lead	

Chapter 4
Pages 82-83 - Study Guide to the Organizing the Elements Brochure

1. G	4. J	7. F	9. A
2. B	5. E	8. C	10. H
3. I	6. D		

Copper:

11. 29
12. Cu
13. 11
14. Transition Elements
15. Solid
16. Metal
17. Natural
18. Stable

Calcium:

35. 20
36. Ca
37. 2
38. Alkaline Earth Metals
39. Solid
40. Metal
41. Natural
42. Stable

Mercury:

19. 80
20. Hg
21. 12
22. Transition Elements
23. Liquid
24. Metal
25. Natural
26. Stable

Uranium:

43. 92
44. U
45. 3
46. Actinides
47. Solid
48. Metal
49. Natural
50. Radioactive

Oxygen:

27. 8
28. O
29. 16
30. BCNO Family
31. Gas
32. Nonmetal
33. Natural
34. Stable

Pages 85-86 - Why Are Elements Put Into Families?

Table 1 -

A. p,p
B. p,p
C. np, np
D. np,np
E. np,np
F. p,p.

Conclusions:

Answers will vary. Here are a few possibilities.

1. Chlorides of alkali metals tend not to precipitate with ammonium compounds. Chlorides of alkali earth metals tend to precipitate with ammonium compounds.
2. Alkali metals, alkaline earth metals, halogens, and BCNO family
3. Alkali metal compounds do not form a precipitate when mixed with ammonium compounds.
4. Alkaline earth metals will form a precipitate when mixed with ammonium compounds.

5. (Table 2)
   Beryllium p,p
   Cesium np,np
   Francium np,np
   Magnesium p,p
   Radium p,p
   Rubidium np, np

Pages 87-88 - The Scientific Method - Why Are Elements Put Into Families Laboratory Quiz

Answers will vary. Here are a few possibilities.

1. How do alkali metals and alkaline earth metals react to ammonium compounds?
2. Alkali metals will form no precipitates where alkaline earth metals will form a precipitate.
3. Safety goggles, aprons, ammonium phosphate, ammonium carbonate, barium chloride, calcium chloride, lithium chloride, potassium chloride, sodium chloride, strontium chloride, test tubes, test tube rack, Barnes bottles, and distilled water
4. Add five drops of barium chloride to a test tube. Add three drops of ammonium carbonate to the barium chloride. Shake the test tube and observe. Record on a data table whether the reaction formed a precipitate or not. Clean the test tube and repeat the experiment, substituting ammonium phosphate for ammonium carbonate. Record the results. Repeat the entire experiment five times, substituting calcium chloride, lithium chloride, potassium chloride, sodium chloride, and strontium chloride for barium chloride.
5. Alkaline earth metals form a precipitate and alkali metals do not.
6. Different families of the periodic table react differently. Members of the same family will react the same.
7. Remaining alkali metals will react the same as lithium, sodium, and potassium.
8. Remaining alkaline earth metals will react the same as barium, calcium, and strontium.
9. The alkali metal compounds and the alkaline earth metal compounds
10. Temperature, volume of chlorides, and ammonium compounds

Page 89 - Families of Elements Poster Activity

Answers will vary depending on the group and family.

Pages 97-98 - The Families of Elements Group Quiz

Part I:

1. Transition elements
2. Noble gases
3. Lanthanides
4. Alkali metals
5. Halogens
6. Actinides
7. BCNO family
8. Alkaline earth metals
9. Actinides
10. BCNO family
11. Transition elements
12. BCNO family
13. Noble gases
14. Halogens
15. Alkali metals
16. Alkaline earth metals

Part II: Answers will vary. Here are a few possibilities.

17. Soda cans
18. Salt
19. Toothpaste
20. Thyroid treatment
21. Balloons
22. Compact discs
23. Nuclear fuel
24. Jewelry
25. Bones and teeth
26. Light bulbs

Part III: Answers will vary. Here are a few possibilities.

27. Fireworks
28. Pipes, wires, coins, cars, and bicycles
29. Flints and glass
30. Light bulbs

Part IV: Answers will vary. Here are a few possibilities.

31. Soft, silvery-white metals
32. High melting points and high densities
33. Good conductors of heat and electricity
34. Metals, nonmetals, and metalloids
35. Combine with alkali metals to form salts
36. Colorless, odorless, and tasteless gases
37. Produce a spark when struck
38. Radioactive

Part V: Answers will vary.

Pages 115-118 - Elements of the Periodic Table Test

Part I. Matching:

1. B
2. T
3. Q
4. I
5. P
6. C
7. F
8. N
9. H
10. E
11. L
12. G

13. O
14. D
15. K
16. R
17. S
18. J
19. A
20. M

Part II. Know Your Symbols:
21. Fe
22. Ca
23. I
24. Mg
25. U
26. K
27. Ag
28. He
29. P
30. C

Part III. Element Families:
31. Noble Gases
32. Actinides
33. Transition elements
34. Alkali metals
35. Lanthanides
36. Alkaline earth metals
37. BCNO group
38. Halogens
39. Transition elements
40. Noble Gases

Part IV. Uses:
Answers will vary. Here are a few possibilities.
41. Soda cans
42. Used in water
43. Light bulbs
44. Computer chips
45. Smoke detectors
46. Lubricants
47. Diamonds
48. Toothpaste
49. Money or jewelry
50. Light bulbs

Part V. Time Line:
Teacher Check. Construction of time lines will vary. Elements should be listed in chronological order.

Part VI. Graphing:
Teacher check. Construction of graphs will vary. Here is one possibility.

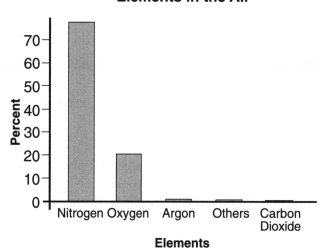

Elements in the Air

Bibliography

Elements and Families

Elements (Science and Nature CD ROM), by Mentorom Multimedia, 1995.

Emsley, John. *The Elements.* Clarendon Press: Oxford, 1989.

Pflaum, Rosalynd. *Marie Curie and Her Daughter Irene.* Learner Publications: Minneapolis, Minnesota, 1993.

Snyder, Carl. *The Extraordinary Chemistry of Ordinary Things,* 2nd ed. Wiley & Sons: New York, New York, 1995.

Swertka, Albert. *A Guide to the Elements,* Oxford, 1996.

Multiple Intelligences

Gardner, Howard. *Multiple Intelligences: The Theory in Practice.* Basic Books, 1993.